LOTUS 123

GW00631050

TEACH YOURSELF BOOKS

Teach Yourself

LOTUS 123
up to version 3.1

David Royall
North Hertfordshire College

Jacky Royall
Barnet College, London

Hodder and Stoughton

A CIP catalogue record for this title is available from the British Library.

ISBN 0 340 55431 2

First published 1991
Reissued 1992
Fifth impression 1993

Typeset by Focal Image Ltd.
Printed in Great Britain for the educational publishing division of
Hodder & Stoughton Ltd, Mill Road, Dunton Green, Sevenoaks, Kent by
Clays Ltd, St Ives plc.

CONTENTS

TEXT DISK

The disk supplied in the book/disk pack contains the spreadsheet files used in the chapters, starting with the sales performance outline spreadsheet used in chapter 2. The disk files used with the chapters do not contain any formulae but are designed to save time setting up the text used in the spreadsheets.

For users with a hard disk system

Before you can use the spreadsheets, you will need to copy them on to your hard disk. To do this follow these instructions:

1   Ensure the Lotus package is installed on your hard disk as explained to you in chapter 1

2   From the operating system prompt (e.g. C:>) ensure you are in the directory where Lotus is stored. To do this type in 'chdir \123R3' to enter the required direcetory. For Release 2 users, the directory where the software is stored on the hard disk is more likely to be \123 rather than \123R3 with Release 3

3   Place the disk into your drive referred to as A:

4   If you are a Release 3 user enter from the keyboard A:R3
     If you are a Release 2 user enter from the keyboard A:R2

5   Now store your disk in a safe place as it will no longer be needed unless you wish to restore the files back to their original state in the future

The appropriate files will have been copied accross for you.

For users with a floppy disk system

Your Lotus system will work on files from the floppy disk. To avoid any accidents, it is wise to make a backup of the disk before you start.

1   Refer to your computer manual about how to make a backup of a disk and then use this to create a copy of the disk

2   Now store the original in a safe place and use the backup. If you need to restore the original files again, repeat the backing up process

3   Whenever you wish to use the files, make sure the floppy disk is in the drive where Lotus looks for the worksheet files (usually the drive denoted as B:)

Gaining access to files

Ensure Lotus is loaded and you are in the spreadsheet option with the mode indicator in the top right-hand corner showing READY.

● Type /F for the menu option File

● Type R to Retrieve a file

A menu of spreadsheets will be displayed. You simply select the spreadsheet by using the right arrow key to highlight the one required. All files relating to the chapters have filenames starting with 'CH' followed by the chapter number and then in sequence to where they appear in the chapter. For example, the file with the name CH5_2 indicates that it is the spreadsheet used in chapter 5, and that it is the second spreadsheet for this chapter.

When the required spreadsheet is highlighted, press ENTER and the spreadsheet will be loaded and you will be returned to the READY mode.

The files named EXAMPLE1, EXAMPLE2 and EXAMPLE3 are example spreadsheets complete with formulae and graphs which you may find useful to work with and make any changes to.

1 GETTING STARTED

1.1 Aims of this chapter

This chapter gives an outline of what Lotus is, what it can do and how you should prepare your computer for its use.

There is also an explanation of some computer terminology that may be new to you. It will help you get started and ensure that you have what is needed to be successful in using the Lotus product.

1.2 What is a spreadsheet?

A spreadsheet is the electronic equivalent of an accountant's ledger - a large piece of paper divided by vertical columns and horizontal rows into a grid of cells. The name derives from the spreading of the organisation's accounts on a sheet of paper and the user can directly enter numbers, formulae or text into the cells.

Screen Dump 1.1 shows what an empty spreadsheet is.

On observing the table you can see that there are letters along the top and numbers down the right side. The highlighted section is known as a cell and is referred to as cell location C5 as indicated in the top left-hand part of the screen. Each cell is referred to by its co-ordinates, like a map reference or point on a graph. Numbers and formulae can be entered into these cells. Once data has been entered in the form of a table, the data can be manipulated. For example formulae can be entered to link cells. An example of linking cells is where a cell entry reads:

B1 * C1

This makes the cell the value of the contents of the cell equal to the cell B1 multiplied by the value of cell C1.

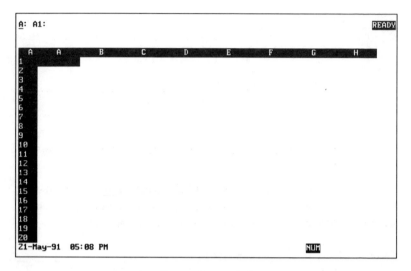

Screen Dump 1.1

The spreadsheet effectively becomes a screen based calculator capable of being printed or displayed as a graph. As a 'tool', accountancy is by no means the only work for which spreadsheets can be used.

Some examples of the power of spreadsheets are:

1 What if? analysis

Any figure can be changed at any time and the new results will be automatically be shown. Thus a What if? analysis might be what if sales were to increase by 10%? The spreadsheet can calculate this easily. It is this facility of being able to re-calculate formulae quickly that makes spreadsheets a powerful, useful and popular analytical tool.

2 Goal seeking

Some spreadsheets are used in order to seek goals. For example, spreadsheets can be set up to depict the sales and costs of a business where a model is set up to determine at what price profits will be maximised.

3 Graphing

In this instance, the spreadsheet is used to represent tables and figures graphically.

4 Storing records of information

A spreadsheet can be used to hold records of information such as details of costs accumulated for a specific job. Such information can be altered quickly and can be used as the basis of a contract tender or for price determination. This type of application is often referred to as one of **database**.

In practice, spreadsheets will be used for a combination of the above. Spreadsheets are flexible modelling tools which can be readily adapted for many jobs involving repetitive numerical calculations.

Some example of use are:

- Financial plans and budgets can be represented as a table, with columns for time periods (e.g. months) and rows for different elements of the plan (e.g. costs and revenue)

- Tax, Investment and Loan calculations.

- Statistics such as averages, standard deviations, time series and regression analysis. Many in-built statistical functions are available in Lotus 123.

- Consolidation – merging branch or departmental accounts to form group (consolidated) accounts. This involves merging two or more spreadsheets together.

- Currency conversion – useful for an organisation with overseas interests.

- Timetabling and Roster planning of staff within organisations or departments.

- In an educational establishment, the recording of class lists, attendance, student marks.

You will probably think of many more potential applications as you work through the book. The name LOTUS comes from the company who manufacture it, and the 123 comes from the three standard applications of Spreadsheet, Database and Graphics. Uses of spreadsheets often combines these three applications.

While working with Lotus, you will often come across the term **worksheet**. This is the name given by Lotus when working with the spreadsheet application and means the same as spreadsheet.

1.3 Hardware and software

Hardware refers to the physical components of a computer system while software refers to the programs that are used to give instructions to the computer. Both are needed if the computer is to achieve anything at all.

Software for a computer will come in many forms; essentially there will be an operating system which will come with the computer system and applications software which you buy as extra. Lotus 123 is an example of applications software.

When the machine is switched on, the computer will need some instructions about how to operate the computer system, hence the term operating system. Different computers will have varying kinds of operating systems which needs to be considered when you are buying applications.

When choosing hardware, you will need to make decisions on such issues as to whether you want a colour screen display, the quality of printer you want, how much storage you need. When selecting software, you are making decisions about what you want your computer to do for you.

It may be the case that you use your computer for more applications than Lotus 123. If this is the case, it is not unusual for the cost of applications software to exceed that of the rest of the system.

1.4 Computer needs

There are now a large range of computer types on the market from which you can choose. Use of the Lotus package tends to be associated with a microcomputer. In other words, a computer that stands by itself and allows one person to sit at a keyboard and operate it. However, there are other types of systems such as networks and multi-user systems on which you will find Lotus being used. If you are buying Lotus, you must know which type of system you will be working with.

1.5 Operating systems

Although all computers appear similar from the outside, they may well have different operating systems. An operating system is the language that any particular machine has to work with, in much the same way that different peoples of the world communicate in different languages.

Most microcomputers use the operating system MSDOS (MicroSoft Disk Operating System). However there are different versions of MSDOS. The different versions have come about because computers have advanced over the years and changes in the operating systems have been required for the new devices to be operated.

Increasingly the operating system OS/2 (Operating System 2) is being used. This has the added advantage over MSDOS in that many 'Jobs' can be executed at the same time. For example, while the computer is printing, an operator can get on with something else without any slowdown in speed. Alternatively, it will allow operators to work on a number of different packages at the same time from one machine.

Network systems require a different operating system again because there is a range of operating systems, it is essential that you check with a supplier that the version of Lotus 123 you buy is the correct version for your computer's operating system.

1.6 Processor types

Part of the computer's hardware is called the processor. All computers need such processing devices as they form the main attributes of a computer system. Over the years such processors have become more sophisticated and more powerful.

Not all software packages will run on all processors, so again, you need to be careful that the software purchased is correct for the machine you have. For example, some versions of Lotus 123 Release 3 will not work on a computer that has a processor with fewer capabilities than that of a 286 type. It is not for a book like this to discuss the varying processor types nor is it necessary for you to know in order to be able to take full advantage of the Lotus package. However, you will need to know if you are going to purchase software.

1.7 Disk drives

Getting a computer with the correct disk drives is important. On microcomputers you normally find two types of disk drive; a floppy disk drive and a hard disk drive.

A hard disk normally comes readily installed into your machine and cannot be removed. It is capable of holding very large amounts of data and is used by the computer when it is running the software. It will be needed to hold the software as well as the spreadsheet data generated.

A floppy disk drive is used to store data on removable small disks. When you receive software, it normally comes on floppy disks. You will then need to copy the data on to the computer's hard disk; clear instructions on how this is achieved will come with the software. Such drives typically require disks of one of two sizes; 3.5 inch or 5.25 inch. When buying software, you will need to advise your dealer as to what size drive you are using.

Some machines have both sizes of drive. Floppy disk drives are also needed for backing up data as a precaution against loss of data.

For both types, the amount of data that can be stored will vary from device to device. Hard disks normally store from 20 megabytes upwards while floppy disks normally store 1 megabyte or less.

It is often difficult to appreciate what a megabyte of data actually is, but to give you some idea, a book of this size, if converted to computerised data, would fit easily on to a 1 megabyte floppy disk.

When software is purchased, it will usually come on a number of floppy disks with most commercial packages taking between 1 and 2 megabytes of storage. Remember, apart from the software storage, your hard disk will also have to store all the data generated by the software.

It is possible to run software on a machine with only floppy disks for storage. Because the normal system in business is at least a hard disk machine or a file server on a network, software has been especially developed to take advantage of this kind of computer power. Therefore, firms are advised that if they are purchasing computer equipment, a hard disk is now essential for most types of business work.

1.8 Screen types

At first sight it may seem that one screen on a computer is very much like any other. However there are now many variations. There is first of all the straight choice of colour and monochrome. Most packages now take advantage of colour, although many users still prefer not to have it.

What will vary is the ability of a screen to do graphics. Screens come with different levels of resolution. The greater the resolution, the better will be the clarity of the picture on the screen. However, having a screen capable of high resolution graphics is still not enough because the computer itself has got to know how to send data to the screen. For this purpose, you will need to be sure that the computer also has an appropriate **graphics** card to go with the screen. The graphics card fits inside the machine and is used by the processor to address the screen.

Lotus will require some graphics capabilities if you are to take advantage of its graphics facilities.

1.9 Printers

You will almost certainly want to print out your spreadsheet. There are many different printers available on the market. However, not all printers will necessarily be able to do what you want. Printers will vary in speed of print, quality of print and paper width (usually 80 column or 132 column width).

Here is a list of some of the main types of printer available and briefly what they can achieve.

Dot matrix printers are the most commonly available type. They have proved to be extremely versatile and can do most jobs. If you are looking for letter quality style print, then you may have to consider 24 pin printers as opposed to 9 pin printers, because a 24 pin printer will print with greater definition. One of the main benefits of using matrix printers is the ability to produce graphics output on them.

Laser printers will give much better output than most dot matrix printers. They work rather like a photocopier by building a complete image of what to print. However, they do cost more and are often restricted in width to standard A4 size.

Daisy Wheel printers will give good quality output but will not print graphics. The characters are placed on a wheel rather than built up with dots in the case of matrix printers.

Ink Jet printers offer good quality output and a low cost method of achieving colour output. Their main drawback tends to be their speed.

Whatever kind of printer is purchased you will need to make sure that Lotus is able send its data to that printer for printing. In practice, it is fairly unlikely that you will select a printer that Lotus is unable to cope with.

1.10 The keyboard

Most keyboards are fairly standard. Before starting, examine your keyboard to determine the whereabouts of the following:

Number pads – On most keyboards there are two sets of number keys from 0 to 9. The reason for this is that some users prefer to use the number pad to the right of the keyboard in the same way they would use a standard calculator. If you do decide to use the number pad, you will need to set the **Num Lock** 'on' when doing so.

Function Keys are especially programmed to perform certain functions. On most keyboards they are either along the top or grouped together on the left-hand side of the keyboard. Each key is normally number F1, F2, F3..., etc. You will, in time, find some of these very useful when using the Lotus package.

Insert, Home, Page Up, Page Down, Delete, End exist on most keyboards and, along with the function keys, offer ways of taking shortcuts. These keys will perform different functions depending upon the package in use. Lotus 123 will make full use of these keys.

Arrow keys (up), (down), (right), (left) often appear as separate function keys on keyboards. If they do not, then you will have to use the ones on the number of your keyboard.

● (multiplication) appears above the 8 key near the top of your keyboard. Unlike the conventional symbol for multiplication it is used in order to avoid confusion with the letter 'x'. Likewise, the / (back slash) key is used for division.

Ctrl (Control) will always be used in conjunction with another key. For example, holding down the Ctrl key and pressing the character 'C' at the same time is used to stop many jobs which are underway such as printing.

ESC (ESCAPE) key is used rather like a function key and is often used, as is the case in Lotus, to 'back track' on a sequence of events or 'undo' an activity.

~ (tilde) is a special key used for the more advanced features of Lotus. It is worth checking its whereabouts on your keyboard.

Alt is used in a similar way to the Ctrl key in that it is pressed simultaneously with other keys. to provide a variety of other facilities.

PrtSc (Print Screen) allows you to 'dump' a copy of the screen to your printer.

/ (**Slash or forward slash**) key is very important when working with Lotus. Try and distinguish it from the \ (backslash key).

\ (**Backslash**) is used as a division symbol in most applications. In Lotus it is also used for more advanced areas of the package.

Getting to know your keyboard is important. However, you will find that if you are new to computing, this will take quite some time and you will need to be patient. Progress can be slow when you are learning a new package such as Lotus and discovering your keyboard at the same time.

1.11 Data storage on disk

It has already been mentioned that data can be stored on hard and floppy disks. Such data, however, has to be organised in a way that can be understood by both the user and the computer. Data will be collected and stored in **files**.

For now, it is simply good enough to know what kind of files data are organised into. There are three types of file that Lotus 123 users need to be concerned with:

1 Operating System files contain the software that the computer needs to instruct it how to operate a system. These files will appear on the hard disk before the Lotus 123 package is ever introduced.

2 Applications software files will be large in number and the process of placing such files on to a hard disk is the installation of the application package.

3 User data will be generated by the package itself. When spreadsheets are made up, the data contained in the spreadsheets are then placed on to the hard disk as files. For each spreadsheet, there will be a distinct file.

Once data are organised into files, the files will have to be located somewhere on the disk. To make file management easy, they can be grouped into directories. The placing of files into directories is largely the user's responsibility. The disk, whether floppy or hard, has a root directory which acts as a starting point from which sub-directories are

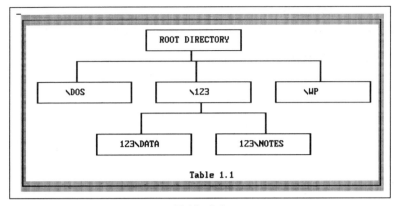

Table 1.1

created and, into which, files are stored. Table 1.1 shows a schematic diagram of how you could organise such a directory structure.

In this table it can be seen that the root directory contains three sub-directories. Assume that Lotus files are stored in the 123 sub-directory. There is no reason why Lotus has to be stored in the 123 directory; you will however, need to know which directory your 123 files are stored in when you want to use them. Files can be held in the root directory or any sub-directory irrespective of whether there are further sub-directories leading from it. Table 1.1 also shows that the 123 sub-directory has two further sub-directories of data and notes.

Organising files in directories is called data management. In many ways, it is no different to organising files in a filing cabinet. The art of good file management is one of knowing where to find information quickly and efficiently.

1.12 Computer memory

Computer memory is the memory which exists inside the computer other than that on disk. Some computer memory is required in order to store programs that are needed to control the computer system – the Operating System. Much more memory is needed for two other main purposes:

1 To hold the application software when it is in use. Lotus is a large software package made up of a large number of separate files all stored on hard disk. Not all of the package is loaded into memory at any one time, only what is needed. Lotus will frequently load files in to memory to instruct it what to do in certain circumstances and then disposing of this from memory when it is no longer required.

2 To hold data generated by the package itself. Again, not all data generated will need to be held in memory at any one time, but will be stored in many separate files and saved on disk.

Computer memory is not of a finite amount – its size is limited. Interacting with files stored on disk allows a computer to extend its capabilities considerably. It is important that when buying software you make sure that your machine has enough memory in the computer itself to copy with the version of Lotus 123 you are buying.

1.13 Menus

You will often come across the Term 'menu' when working with computers. A menu is simply a list of options that you can choose from. Quite often, when selecting a menu option you are given yet more options from that option – a sub-menu. This hierarchical structure of menus is now very common among applications on computers. In practice, the successful use of computer software often largely rests with the operator knowing the way around a set of menus.

Lotus is no exception to using such menu structures. A good deal of your effort in teaching yourself Lotus will be in finding your way around the Lotus menu structure.

As mentioned before, there are now different versions of the Lotus package. Later versions tend to have a greater number of facilities. Lotus have managed to keep the original style and philosophy of the spreadsheet (or worksheet) handling. They have achieved this largely by adding the extra functions and inserting more options into the menu structure. This has the clear advantage that if you move from one version of Lotus to another, you will be familiar with the style and may only need to learn some new options. In fact, when 'upgrading' from one version of Lotus to another (say from Release 2.01 to Release 3.1) all the data files generated in the earlier version can be used in the newer version.

1.14 Installing Lotus 123

When your software arrives you will receive:

- A number of floppy disks containing your software

- A reference manual

- A tutorial manual

- A set of instruction booklets one of which is an instruction book on setting up Lotus 123

If your hard disk has been prepared in the correct way then the whole process of installing Lotus on to a hard disk has been made a little easier by Lotus as they supply an installation program on one of the floppy disks. What the installation program will achieve is to place the required files on floppy disks on to your hard disk in the correct directories.

Assuming you have a hard disk system or are using a network, then to install the software all you need to do is:

- Switch your computer on.

- Place the disk marked installation into your floppy disk drive. If you have two drives, then it should go into the one you refer to as A: drive.

- From the operating system prompt type 'A:' in order to be able to access the files on the floppy disk where the Lotus install program is held.

- Now type 'INSTALL' to start installation.

- A set of instructions will appear on your screen requiring you to enter the company or owner details.

When a package is purchased, it is done so on the understanding that it is for that company or person only. You are simply being asked to state who the rightful owner of the property is.

The rest of the installation procedure will ask:

- what operating system your system uses.

- what disk drives on your computer are being used and the directory where the Lotus programs are to be stored.

- what screen and graphics you have.

- what printer(s) is being used on your computer.

Follow the instructions as they appear; they are largely self explanatory. You will need to have all the other disks at hand.

Eventually you will leave the installation program and will find yourself back at the operating system.

If you have installed the software incorrectly, then you can always re-install it. To do this make sure you are in the correct directory (see the next section about how to achieve this) and enter 'INSTALL'. When you want to install your software again or wish to make some alterations you will not necessarily need to use all the floppy disks again; this is because much of the software will already be on your hard disk.

1.15 Getting started

With the diversity of operating systems and the different versions of Lotus 123, it is very difficult to give precise instructions about installing the package in a book like this. However, once installed, the rest is a little more straightforward.

To get started you will need to make sure you are working from the directory where Lotus is stored on the hard disk. To do this you will need to:

- Enter 'C:' on the operating system to ensure you are on Drive C (the hard disk). On some computers your hard disk may be something other than drive C.

- Type in 'chdir \123R3' to enter the required directory. For Release 2 users, the directory where the software is stored on the hard disk, is more likely to be \123 rather than \123R3 with Release 3.

- Enter LOTUS and you will see the Access System menu on your screen.

Screen dump 1.2 shows the Access menu for Release 3 while screen dump 1.3 shows the Release 2 Access menu. In both cases, the menu option 1-2-3 is highlighted when started up.

From observation, you will see that releases have an INSTALL option. This is used to change any information about your computer system; e.g. adding a different printer or correcting an installation error. Likewise, both Releases have a Translate facility which is used to convert other spreadsheets into a form that this version of Lotus can handle.

The Exit option will return you to the operating system.

For Release 2 users there are the added options of View and Printgraph. View offers a screen orientated demonstration on how to use Lotus 123 while Printgraph is used to print graphs created by spreadsheets. These options are not required by Release 3 users as they are embedded within the 1-2-3 option.

- Select option 1-2-3 by ensuring the option is highlighted and then press the Return or ENTER key

This will be the future procedure for entering the spreadsheet.

If you are working on a network system then the approach may be different in that an opening menu may appear for you with the option of the Lotus package being available.

```
 The Lotus spreadsheet integrating 3-D worksheets, graphics, and database
 1-2-3        Install        Translate      Exit
```

```
                              Lotus
                       1-2-3 Access Menu

                           Release 3
           Copyright 1989 Lotus Development Corporation
                     All Rights Reserved.




 To select a program to start, highlight the menu item using →, ←, HOME,
 or END and press ENTER, or press the first character of the item.

 Press F1 for more information.

                                                           NUM
```

Screen Dump 1.2

```
 1-2-3  PrintGraph  Translate  Install  View  Exit
 Enter 1-2-3 -- Lotus Worksheet/Graphics/Database program
```

```
                         1-2-3 Access System
                    Lotus Development Corporation
                           Copyright 1985
                         All Rights Reserved
                             Release 2

 The Access System lets you choose 1-2-3, PrintGraph, the Translate utility,
 the Install program, and A View of 1-2-3 from the menu at the top of this
 screen.  If you're using a diskette system, the Access System may prompt
 you to change disks.  Follow the instructions below to start a program.

 o  Use [RIGHT] or [LEFT] to move the menu pointer (the highlight bar at
    the top of the screen) to the program you want to use.

 o  Press [RETURN] to start the program.

 You can also start a program by typing the first letter of the menu
 choice.  Press [HELP] for more information.

                         Press [NUM LOCK]
```

Screen Dump 1.3

Before progressing to the next chapter it is suggested you make quite
certain that you know how to enter your particular version of Lotus on
your computer; variations on getting started can be considerable.

1.16 Chapter Summary

In this chapter, you have covered the following points

● what a spreadsheet is and what it can do

● what software is and what hardware is needed to run Lotus 123

● the way data are stored in files and how directory listings are used to give us details about the nature of files

● how a hierarchical directory structure can be used to manage the file storage on a disk

● how to install Lotus on to a hard disk and subsequently how to get started with Lotus 123

2 STARTING WITH SPREADSHEETS

2.1 Aims of this chapter

The aim of this chapter is to help you get some idea of what a spreadsheet does and its style of operation. Most activities will be by example and you are encouraged to extend the examples as a way of investigating the capabilities of the Lotus 123 package.

To begin with, it is assumed that you have installed your Lotus 123 package on to your machine. If you have not done so, then refer to the section in chapter 1 on installing your software.

2.2 Getting Started

- Switch on and boot up the computer

- Type 'LOTUS' and wait for the Lotus system to be loaded into main memory.

- The menu line should display the Access System Command menu with 1-2-3 highlighted.

- Press the ENTER key (Return on some keyboards) to select 123 which is the spreadsheet option. Some keyboards will not have either ENTER or RETURN on them, so please check which key is referred to as Return.

The display screen

Examine screen dump 2.1.

The empty spreadsheet you start off with will vary slightly according to the version of Lotus that you are working with.

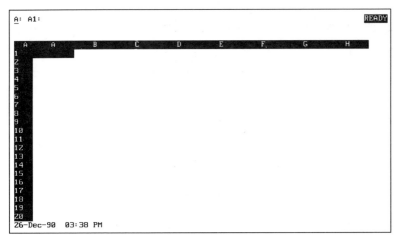

A: A1:   READY

| A | B | C | D | E | F | G | H |

1
2
3
4
5
6
7
8
9
10
11
12
13
14
15
16
17
18
19
20
26-Dec-90   03:38 PM

Screen Dump 2.1

The control panel

The top three lines form the control panel. You will find that, although your spreadsheet data is not placed in this section, the control panel will prove vital to you.

If you are using Version 3, then the panel will show on the top line, 'A:A1' in the left corner and 'READY' in the right corner. This indicates that you are in spreadsheet A at cell location A1 and the computer is ready for input. If the prefix of 'A:' does not show and only 'A1' appears then it is simply telling you are at cell location A1. Earlier versions of Lotus only allow you to work on one spreadsheet at a time.

The second line is where you will see your typing. If 123 prompts you to input data you will see it here. Menu selections are displayed on the second line also.

A third line is 123's comment line for messages such as sub-menus and instructions. The use of this line will become apparent fairly soon.

2.3   Columns and rows _____

The letters that appear across the screen indicate the column title, A,B,C etc., while the numbers down the left side indicate row titles. The highlighted part of the screen is situated at location Column A Row 1, referred to as CELL A1. This is the method by which cells are referred to.

Locate the arrow keys on the keyboard → right arrow key, ← left arrow key, ↑ up arrow key, ↓ down arrow key

- Press the down arrow key twice and the right arrow key once.

This should now leave you at cell location B3. Look at the control panel to confirm this. Also the cell should be highlighted.

- Press the Home key to return to cell location A1.

The entire spreadsheet is normally too large to fit onto your screen because there are 256 columns (lettered A–Z, AA–BZ up to IV) and 8192 rows (numbered 1...8192). However, it is easy to move to any part of the spreadsheet that you need to get to. On some machines, the number of rows may only go as far as 2048.

The rectangular bar that highlights the position of the current cell is called the **cell pointer**.

2.4   Moving around the spreadsheet _____

The pointer can be moved from cell to cell with cursor control (arrow) keys as shown. However, pressing F5 and typing the cell address, e.g. 'D12', will enable you to jump straight to any specified cell location within the spreadsheet.

The **Home** key returns you to the top left-hand corner of your spreadsheet which is cell location A1. You can jump a screen (page) at a time by using these keys;

PgUp	Moves one screen up
PgDn	Moves one screen down
Tab	Move right
Shift/Tab	moves left (Press both keys simultaneously)

Moving the cell pointer off the end of the displayed spreadsheet either vertically or horizontally is known as **scrolling**. As you scroll so new columns or row labels will appear and others will disappear. However, you will always be able to get back to them; information out of sight will not be lost.

Another useful key to help you get around your spreadsheet is the End key; you use it in conjunction with one other key. If you press the End key followed by the down arrow key you will go down to the end of the spreadsheet to Row 8192. If you press End followed by the right arrow key you will go to the far right of the screen to column IV. In most cases you will not want to move to the extreme corners of your spreadsheet. However, by pressing the Shift and right arrow key simultaneously, you will move to the far right of your screen. This principle is the same for left, down and up.

File and Clock Indicator

If you are working on a file that has either been saved or one that has been retrieved from a disk, then its name and location on your disk will appear in the bottom left-hand corner of your screen. If no file has been saved, then the current date and time will appear instead.

The size of your spreadsheet

To put the size of a spreadsheet into some perspective, we can establish that there are a total of 8192 rows numbered 1 to 8192 and 256 columns labelled A,B,C...Z,AA,AB..AZ,BA,BB...IV. This gives a total of 2,097,152 cells in total. The next step is to decide what can go into these cells.

- Experiment with moving around the spreadsheet using the various methods outlined.

● Get to the **home** position at cell **A1** and press the left arrow key. The beep sound tells you that you cannot move outside the range of the spreadsheet.

You might find yourself having to refer back to these pages as you work through the rest of this chapter, but now it is time to make a start on entering something for yourself.

2.5 Entering Text

To begin with you can enter one of three types of data into a cell:

ANumber —data which can be used in calculations

—must start with a number; 0...9 + − / * . $

—Scientific notation (e.g. 1.23 E+06)

—may end with a per cent sign (%)

A Formula —Mathematical formulae or functions that compute values

—Lotus has many built-in functions for statistical, financial and other work; they begin with the @ sign (e.g. @SUM(B4..F4) adds all the numbers in the cells B4 through F4)

Please Note: The * (Asterisk) sign indicates multiplication when it appears within formula

A Label —Titles or text in alphanumeric characters which makes the information understandable

—Can contain any string, characters or numbers

—May start with any character accept those which indicate a number or a formula or are otherwise used by Lotus such as the / sign

—May be up to 240 characters long

—May display across several spreadsheet columns. If the next column is occupied, 123 displays as many characters as possible and stores the rest.

—To ensure a label, make the first letter a Label Prefix. Such labels will position the text in the cell and allow the use of special characters otherwise not permitted:

'	(Apostrophe)	Left justify text. Is default if no prefix is used
"	(Double quote)	right justify
^	(Caret)	Centre
\	(Back slash)	Repeat text across cell

There are other entry types which you will learn about later on in the book when such details are needed.

You should now be faced with an empty spreadsheet, with the cell in the top left-hand corner highlighted by the Cell Cursor.

Any entry you make will be typed on the second line of the screen and will be put into the cursor when you press Enter. Making sure you are in the Home position (top left-hand corner, cell A1) proceed with the instructions that follow.

● Type 'FIRST DEMONSTRATION' and press Enter.

● Press the down arrow key twice and type 'PRICE' and Press the down arrow key. Note how this last action entered the text AND moved down to the next cell.

● Type 'COST' and press the down arrow key.

● Type 'PROFIT' and press the right arrow key. At this point the cursor should be in cell B5.

Such entries of TEXT are known in Lotus 123 as LABELS. You will no doubt have noticed that these labels always appear in the far left-hand side of the cell. You should now have the screen display as in screen dump 2.2

You should be able to see on the screen that the label 'FIRST DEMONSTRATION' has been written across two cells. This is permissible only because no text appears in the adjoining cell B1.

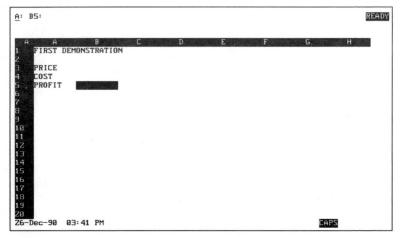

```
A: B5:                                                    READY

   A        A          B        C       D       E       F       G       H
1    FIRST DEMONSTRATION
2
3    PRICE
4    COST
5    PROFIT
6
7
8
9
10
11
12
13
14
15
16
17
18
19
20
26-Dec-90  03:41 PM                                              CAPS
```

Screen Dump 2.2

2.6 Correcting errors

However careful you are, mistakes are going to be made. There are two ways of correcting a mistake. Suppose that the entry 'FIRST DEMONSTRATION' was meant to be 'First Demonstration'. To alter it you go to cell A1 and type in the correct version, making no attempt to delete the old text from the cell. Alternatively go to cell A1 and press F2. In the control panel the text 'FIRST DEMONSTRATION' should appear. Now:

• Keep pressing the Back arrow key (erase) until you delete up to the 'F'.

• Now enter the correct text and press RETURN.

When the text appears in the control panel in this way, you can also use the right and left arrow keys to move across the cell contents to correct small parts of it. This technique can be time saving when cell entries are large or are extremely complex as with long formulae. It means you do not have to type the whole entry.

2.7 Entering Numbers _____

Lotus distinguishes between VALUES and LABELS simply by what the first character begins with. If the first character is a number (0–9), then a value is assumed while if the first character is a letter (a–z OR A–Z) then a label is assumed. Hence, if you enter 'Over 18 years of age' a label is assumed. If, however, you wanted to enter the text '18 years and over' as a label, then you would need to place ' (apostrophe) into the cell as the first character otherwise it would be assumed to be a value.

- Now enter numbers in the cells B3 and B4. Enter 58 in cell B3 and 50 in cell B4.

Such numeric entries in Lotus are called VALUE entries.

2.8 Entering a Formula _____

- Type '+B3-B4' in cell B5 and press Enter. You have just entered a FORMULA.

The result of the calculation i.e. 58–50, should appear in cell B5. From screen dump 2.3 you will observe that the result of the formula appears in cell B5 while the formula of cell B5 appears on the top line of the control panel.

Lotus distinguishes formulae from labels and values by the use of the + appearing as the first character in the cell entry. This can also be achieved by placing the whole formula between brackets. In other words, this could be just as effective if the formula was entered as (b3+b4). You will also note that the use of both upper case and lower case can be used in formulae.

- To practice this go to cell b3 and enter a different number and observe the result. Do the same to cell b4.

You now have a spreadsheet with LABELS (in A1, A3 and A4), VALUES (in B3 and B4) and a FORMULA to be evaluated (in B5). On a very small scale this is what spreadsheets are all about!! Try altering the price and cost cells, using arrow keys to position the cell

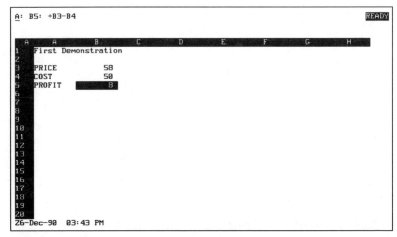

Screen Dump 2.3

cursor followed by typing in a value and Enter to insert it. Before going further, experiment by creating more cell entries with extra formulae. For example, add a new cell that shows the profit percentage over selling price (B5/B3*100).

The following characters are use in formula:

+	Add
–	Subtract
*	Multiply
/	Divide
(	Open bracket (round bracket only)
)	Close bracket (round bracket only)

Building up a formula in Lotus conforms to all the normal rules of mathematical formula.

2.9 Saving your work

In order to save the spreadsheet you need to locate the Lotus MENU. This offers a list of the Lotus Commands available. Such commands will be needed to perform a whole host of functions. Plenty will be said on this throughout the book.

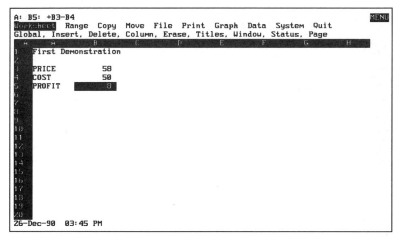

Screen Dump 2.4

- Press the / (slash) key then look at the menu that appears at the top of the screen.

Please note that there should be two slash keys on your keyboard; \ (backslash) will not have the same effect. The menu that appears is shown in Screen Dump 2.4

On the top line of the menu you will observe that the word 'Worksheet' is highlighted. On the second line is a list of options within this main menu command of Worksheet. What you want from the list of commands is the option File. Getting to this option can be achieved in one of two ways:

- Pressing the first letter of the command option, 'F'

- or highlighting the option by pressing the right arrow key. In this instance you will need to press it four times. Press the right arrow key until File is highlighted.

At this point you should see the options available within the file command as shown in screen dump 2.5.

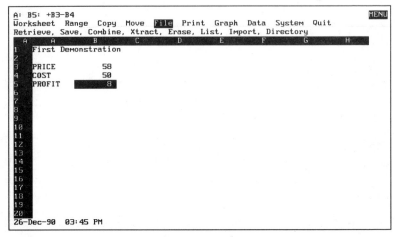

```
A: B5: +B3-B4                                              MENU
Worksheet  Range  Copy  Move  File  Print  Graph  Data  System  Quit
Retrieve, Save, Combine, Xtract, Erase, List, Import, Directory
     A        B        C        D        E        F        G        H
 1 First Demonstration
 2
 3 PRICE           58
 4 COST            50
 5 PROFIT           8
 6
 7
 8
 9
10
11
12
13
14
15
16
17
18
19
20
26-Dec-90  03:45 PM
```

Screen Dump 2.5

Again, the Lotus command is made up of a series of sub-commands which will be reflected in the hierarchical menu structure.

● With the cursor over File, press ENTER.

● Now use the arrow key to highlight Save and press ENTER again.

You will now be asked for a file name On the top of your screen will be the words; 'Enter name of file to save: C:\123\'

The prefix 'C:' indicates the drive the file is to be saved on while '\123\' indicates the directory. These concepts were referred to in chapter 1. The prefix on your machine may well differ from this. Do not worry; it simply means that Lotus will have been configured differently for your machine.

● Enter, for example's sake, the name firstgo and press the Enter key again.

You will now have saved your work on to a disk which can be retrieved at a later point in time. When you learn to develop some sophisticated spreadsheets that take a long time to prepare, you will soon realise that it is always a good idea to save your work periodically. The purpose of doing this is that should anything ever go wrong, you will still be able to retrieve some of your work without having to start from scratch. More will be said about this at later stages.

2.10 Printing your work

To complete the process, you can print the spreadsheet. If you do not have a printer attached, then skip this section.

● Recall your menu using the '/' key and select the MENU command. Print by using the right arrow key to highlight the word.

In time all the print options will be explained. For now you will use the shortest and easiest way.

● Select Printer from this menu to indicate that you want output to be sent to a printer and not to a file.

You should now have on your second and third control panel lines the Print options and another sub-menu respectively with Range highlighted.

● Select Range and you will see the prompt appear:

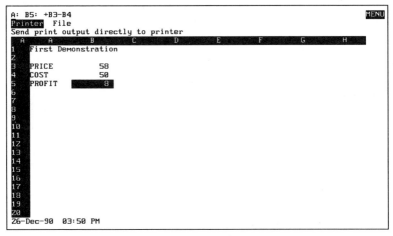

Screen Dump 2.6

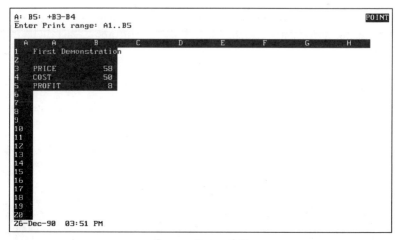

```
A: B5: +B3-B4                                            POINT
Enter Print range: A1..B5
    A      A        B      C      D      E      F      G      H
1       First Demonstration
2
3       PRICE          58
4       COST           50
5       PROFIT          8
6
7
8
9
10
11
12
13
14
15
16
17
18
19
20
26-Dec-90   03:51 PM
```

Screen Dump 2.7

'Enter Range to Print:'

● Enter the range 'A1..B5'

The effect of this is to tell the computer to print everything enclosed in the rectangle formed with A1 at one corner and B5 at the other.

Screen Dump 2.7 shows the effect of a highlighted range which needs to be achieved if the desired range is to be printed.

● Make sure your printer is ready and select Go from the Print menu as shown in screen dump 2.6 earlier

This should have activated the printer and a print of your work should be ready. Meanwhile, on the screen you will be returned to the spreadsheet and in the READY mode. If an error has occurred, then it is probably because your printer has not been switched on or connected.

If you have not been able to follow all of this or feel unable to remember how everything was achieved, then do not worry. You will get further help and practice as you work through the book.

You will now have performed the typical process involved in produced a spreadsheet, namely;

1   Load a spreadsheet.

2   Prepare a spreadsheet with Labels, Formulae and Values.

3   Enter a varied number of values to see what the results would be.

4   Save it.

5   Print it.

2.11 Erasing data from a spreadsheet _____

To start a new spreadsheet you first need to Erase the existing one.

● Move the Cell cursor to A1 (Home position). This can be achieved on most machines by pressing the 'home' key.

● Type '/' to call up the menu, then 'R' for range followed by 'E' for erase.

You are now being asked for the range of cells you want to delete. Since you have placed the cursor in cell A1, 123's suggestion of A1 as the top of the left-hand corner of the range is acceptable.

● Type '.' (full stop) to ANCHOR this corner then use the arrow keys to move the cursor to the bottom right of the spreadsheet.

This is a technique that can be used to set a range on which to act. In some cases it may be quicker to type in the range 'A1..B5' which was the technique suggested when selecting a range to be printed.

This should have highlighted everything we want to delete in inverse video. This principle of ANCHORING is an important one which will be referred to many more times in this book. Make sure you have highlighted all of the spreadsheet you want erased.

● Press ENTER and the sheet will be cleared.

Exactly the same thing could have been achieved by selecting from the menu the option Worksheet. In this menu is the option Delete which deletes the whole spreadsheet. Although it does not require you

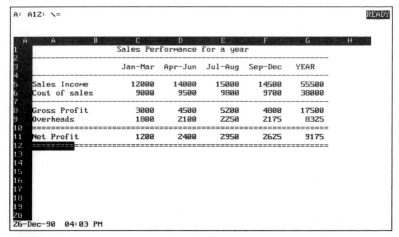

Screen Dump 2.8

to select a range to erase, it will ask you whether you are sure that is what you want.

2.12 A new spreadsheet – Sales Performance _____

Having got this far it is now time to try and create a spreadsheet similar to that shown in screen dump 2.8.

The text and some of the figures will have to be typed in, but if the spreadsheet is to have any advantages over a word processor, we must be sure to ask the computer to do the calculations for us rather than simply entering the results of formula in.

When working through this exercise, you might find it useful to enter the first letter of the menu commands rather than to highlight what is wanted. In some of our instructions this is suggested. However, keep a close eye on what is actually happening.

- Type in all the labels (the text), putting Jan-Mar in cell C3, Apr-Jun into D3 and so on. Then on rows 5 and 6, enter the eight sales and cost figures.

If you want to enter text into a cell and centre it in the cell, rather than leave it justified, enter the cell label starting with the '^' sign rather than just typing it into the cell.

Given that overheads are 20% of sales, all the empty spaces can be filled in by calculation, i.e. by Lotus itself. You have to instruct Lotus about the calculations.

- Gross Profit for Jan–Mar sales is Sales less Costs. Enter the formula '+C5-C6' into cell C8.

For cell columns headed Apr–Jun, Jul–Aug and Sep–Dec you can use Lotus Copy command.

- From the MENU that appears select Copy.

You will now be asked what cells you want to Copy. In fact you are going to copy a formula that is in cell C8 into each of the cells D8, E8 and F8.

- At the prompt 'From', enter the range 'C8..C8'.

Although you are copying from just one cell, it is still important to enter a complete range.

- At the prompt 'To', enter the range 'D8..F8'

- Overheads for Jan-Mar are 20% of Sales. Enter '+C5*0.15%' into cell C9. The use of the percentage (%) sign will instruct the computer to multiply by 20 and then divide by 100 to give 20%.

- For the cell columns headed Apr–Jun, Jul–Aug and Sep–Dec Enter:- '/Copy' from 'C9..C9' to 'D9..F9' in the same way as explained earlier.

If you are unclear about what has happened, then give yourself time to experiment at this stage. What you have just done is going to be fundamental to making spreadsheets quick and easy to set up.

You should be able to work out how to handle the Net Profit. From the spreadsheet it will be (gross profit) – (overheads).

You can now calculate totals to give the YEAR figure. For this you will use a Lotus function rather than a formula. This function represents a fourth type of cell entry.

- In G5 enter '@SUM(C5..F5)'. This saves typing +C5+D5+... etc. After this Copy the function downwards, this time into G5..G11.

All functions start with the '@' sign followed by the function name (SUM in this example) with a range of cells in brackets. As an alternative to this, you could have used a very long formula to add up each cell entry. Although this might suffice with only a few cells, it will prove extremely tedious if you had to add the contents of more than, say, 20 cell values.

As a conclusion to this example, tidy up the spreadsheet by:

a Centring the column headings of Jan–Mar, Apr–Jun, Jul–Aug, Sep–Dec and YEAR.

b Inserting the dotted lines. If you enter either '\=' or '\-', it has the effect of copying either the '=' or '-' across the cell. From here, practise using the copy command to get a line across the spreadsheet.

Now make sure the spreadsheet is saved under the name **profits** using the command '/FSPROFITS'.

Having saved this, you can now either clear the spreadsheet from memory leaving you with a blank spreadsheet in preparation for another exercise or quit the spreadsheet altogether (see below).

Quitting your spreadsheet

- Call up your menu using '/'.

- Now select the option Quit.

At this point you are being asked whether you are sure you want to quit Lotus altogether. This is simply making you think twice about what you are doing. When leaving the package in this way, if your spreadsheet has not been saved, it will be lost permanently.

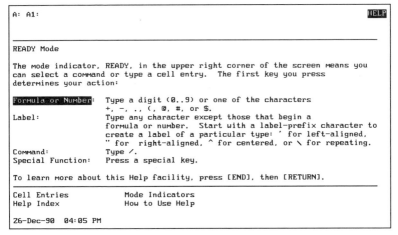

```
A: A1:                                                                    HELP

READY Mode

The mode indicator, READY, in the upper right corner of the screen means you
can select a command or type a cell entry.  The first key you press
determines your action:

Formula or Number:  Type a digit (0..9) or one of the characters
                    +, -, ., (, @, #, or $.
Label:              Type any character except those that begin a
                    formula or number.  Start with a label-prefix character to
                    create a label of a particular type: ' for left-aligned,
                    " for right-aligned, ^ for centered, or \ for repeating.
Command:            Type /.
Special Function:   Press a special key.

To learn more about this Help facility, press [END], then [RETURN].

Cell Entries              Mode Indicators
Help Index                How to Use Help

26-Dec-90  04:05 PM
```

Screen Dump 2.9

- As you will have saved your spreadsheet answer 'Yes' to the question and you will be returned to the Lotus Front menu.

- From here, Exit to return to the operating system.

Asking for HELP

At any time while working through a spreadsheet, Lotus offers you various levels of help. To get help press function key F1 on your key board. Look at screen dump 2.9. It is the HELP screen you get when you are in the READY mode. It gives you some basic instructions about what the cells are and how you can get under way with Lotus.

- Call up the Lotus menu with the / (slash) key and then call for help.

You should now have something similar to Screen Dump 2.10.

Screen Dump 2.10 gives you basic details about what each menu option is for. The essence of the help function is that Lotus knows where you are at any given point and will show a help screen that is applicable to where you are. This is what is meant by help levels. Use this as often as possible; it will serve well as a way of reinforcing your understanding.

```
A: A1:                                                          HELP
Worksheet  Range  Copy  Move  File  Print  Graph  Data  System  Quit
Global, Insert, Delete, Column, Erase, Titles, Window, Status, Page
─────────────────────────────────────────────────────────────────────
1-2-3 Commands

Select a command from the menu on the second line of the control panel or
press [ESCAPE] to return to READY mode.

1-2-3 commands establish overall procedures: copy, move, and delete data in
the worksheet; change numeric formats; transfer data to and from disk storage;
print your work; draw graphs; handle databases; and let you leave 1-2-3:

/Worksheet        /Move          /Graph         /Quit
/Range            /File          /Data
/Copy             /Print         /System


To cancel a command and back up one step, press [ESCAPE].

To cancel a command and return to READY mode, press [BREAK].

─────────────────────────────────────────────────────────────────────
Command Menus          Help Index
26-Dec-90  04:05 PM
```

Screen Dump 2.10

2.13 Summary

In this chapter, you have covered the following points:

- Loading Lotus into your computer and understanding the opening screen display

- Identifying the function of the control panel and the layout of cells into columns and rows

- Identifying some of the different categories of cell entries; Labels, Values, Formula and Functions

- Entering various data types to the spreadsheet

- Examining and find your way around Lotus menus

- Saving and printing files

- Erasing data from a worksheet

- Copying formula across a range of cells

- Using various levels of Lotus HELP

- Quitting the Lotus package

3 MENUS, PRINTING AND FILING

3.1 Aims of this chapter

One of the principle features of getting to know any package is being able to find your way around a menu system. Lotus is no exception to this. It has a hierarchical structure of menus which are quite extensive. This chapter will make you familiar with this structure and help you understand the main options you will commonly need when using the spreadsheet.

In describing the menu system, emphasis has been placed on Saving and Retrieving files to and from your disk as well as being able to print your spreadsheet.

Although these were all introduced in chapter 2, this chapter investigates these facilities in much more detail.

The last chapter of the book has tree diagrams that lay out the menu structure of Lotus in more detail. After working through this chapter, you may well find this a useful reference for future activities.

3.2 Using 123's Menus

You can select from a list of choices (command menus) displayed in the control panel.

- Menus have a multi-level structure. Only one level at a time is shown; more than one selection may often be necessary.

- There are two methods of choosing an item.

- The first and safest method is to POINT by using the cursor movement; the other is to TYPE the first letter of the command, which is much quicker.

- The ESC (ESCAPE) key is used to return to the previous menu and has the effect of undoing the last command.

- You can request main menu by pressing the '/' (slash) key.

Selection will cause changes in the control panel. A new menu will appear on the second line and new commands on the third line. You can continue to make selections or use the **ESC** key to return.

More than one menu selection represents a **command sequence**. In order to gain some practice, get into your spreadsheet and enter the data into the cells as shown in screen dump 3.1

3.3 Saving a file

At this stage, do not worry if your spreadsheet has a different format to the one shown. The only data that exist in this spreadsheet are labels and values.

In order to save your work press '/FS' and then enter the file name 'STORE' followed by pressing Return.

```
A:A13: 'TOTALS                                                    READY

   A        A         B         C        D         E        F         G        H
   SALES FIGURES FOR XYZ STORES LTD
1
2
3                   Cosmetics  Mens     Ladies   Childrens
4                              Wear     Wear     Wear      TOTALS
5
6  Monday          244.89    123.11   133.99    89.99
7  Tuesday         233.1     213.5    222.89    78.67
8  Wednesday       222       178      154.91    69
9  Thursday        301.12    322.92   243       108
10 Friday          278.19    244.67   287.9     120.2
11 Saturday        401.67    398.68   480       275
12
13 TOTALS
14
15
16
17
18
19
20
27-Oct-90   01:29 PM
```

Screen Dump 3.1

■ 38

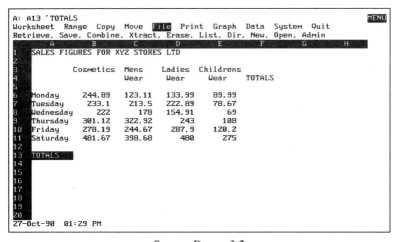

Screen Dump 3.2

Now repeat this process, but instead of pressing the keys, POINT to the command using your arrow keys or mouse. To do this, select the menu by depressing the '/'.

Screen dump 3.2 illustrates the menu structure from the main Lotus menu with the File option highlighted in the second Row of the control panel. The third Row shows the next sequence for filing.

● Use the down arrow key to highlight the word 'file' and press Return.

From the main menu, you should have found your way to the sub-menu of the file command.

● Now highlight the word Save and press Return.

This happens to be the end of the sequence. Some required actions involve more than two commands.

● At this point enter the file name 'STORE' again and press Return.

The system should now be warning that a file already exists on the disk with the same name.

● Highlight Replace and press Return.

By entering Replace, you will have overwritten the old file with the same name as this one. In the case above they are exactly the same, so no changes will have been made. In future, you will need to ensure you have different file names. For example, having called this file 'STORE' you might want to save an updated version of this without losing the original; saving with another name such as 'STORE2' will mean you can keep both versions.

3.4 **Retrieving a file**

As an exercise, delete the existing spreadsheet and then retrieve the file back from the disk. If you have failed to save your work properly, then you will find yourself having to start from scratch.

● Call up the Lotus menu again and select Worksheet.

● Now select Quit and answer 'Yes' to the question indicating that you are sure you want to quit.

At this stage the file is no longer in the computer memory. However, the file should have been placed on disk.

● Now recall your Lotus menu and select the File option.

● From the menu select Retrieve.

The third line of the control panel should now reveal all the spreadsheet files available in the current directory. screen dump 3.3 illustrates such an example.

The second line of the control panel simply indicates where the current file pointer is situated. It also indicates the current directory and disk where files are located. The third line shows you what files are available.

● Press the right arrow key to find what you want to retrieve.

● When you have highlighted the file name 'STORE', press the Return key and the file should now reappear.

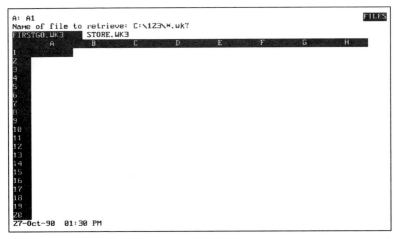

Screen Dump 3.3

3.5   The menu structure

Before progressing further, it is worth examining the command sequence that you have just encountered. Look at table 3.1.

By examining this tree diagram, you will be able to observe the route taken in order to achieve the objectives of either saving a file or

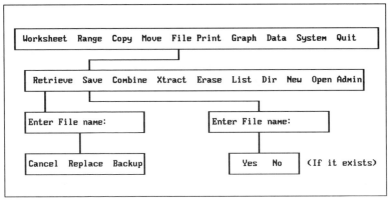

Table 3.1

retrieving one. In chapter 12 there is a collection of such tree diagrams to assist you in finding your way around the Lotus menus. Although many command sequences will soon become familiar with you, there are some that are so infrequently used that you will have difficulty in remembering them without the aid of such diagrams.

Being sure of what you are doing

Screeen dump 3.4 shows, at the foot of the 'tree', questions that may be asked of you. This is a normal feature of the Lotus package which is warning you that data is about to be altered. In the case of saving a file, it has already been indicated that the question whether you want the existing file on the disk replaced with the one in memory only occurs if that file name already exists.

In the case of retrieving a file, a possibility of three choices can arise if you are retrieving a file while a spreadsheet is still on your screen. Lotus will warn you that if the spreadsheet data on the disk is loaded to your screen, then it is replaced by the disk version, meaning you will lose the current version if you have not previously saved it on your disk. On the other hand you are given the option of backup which will allow you to place the current screen file on disk with another file name before loading the new spreadsheet into memory. Using the cancel option simply returns you to your existing spreadsheet without loading into memory a new one.

We shall return to this issue of filing, but for now we shall examine the menus further and look at ways of printing our work.

3.6 Printing your work

From the Lotus menu, the Print commands will let you create printed copies of a worksheet. Check that your printer is properly configured and switched on with paper correctly aligned.

On selecting the Print command you will then need to select Printer to indicate that output is to go to a printer. Once selected you will have to specify the Range you want printed before printing can start.

To demonstrate the principle, try the following:

- Call the menu up and select Print.

- You will now have a number of options depending on the version of Lotus you are working with. Select the Printer option to indicate that you want output to go to a printer.

At this stage you are being asked to specify what part of the spreadsheet to print. This facility is important because there are many instances where you do not require an entire spreadsheet to be printed. When selecting a portion of the spreadsheet to print, you can either use the technique of pointing, anchoring and highlighting what you want printed or typing in the range required. Print the entire spreadsheet for now.

- Specify the range 'A1..F13'.

- Now use the option Go to start printing.

Print options include the ability to insert headers and footers on each page, align margins, print borders, specify font size and style of print and set the page length. Rather than printing straight away, it is possible to save print files to disk. Files can then be printed later from DOS or used in other programs such as word processing. We shall return to printing when we have built up the spreadsheet a little more.

3.7 Editing cells

If a cell entry is incorrect or needs updating, just retype it and overwrite the original entry. In many instances the edit facility F2 provides a quick way of changing entries. When pressing F2, cell entry contents will appear on the second line of the control panel. Cursor keys can be used to move around the entry. The Del key deletes the character at the cursor, the Backspace key deletes the character preceding the cursor. The Ins key switches between inserting text by moving existing text to the right and replacing existing text. Hit the Return key when editing is complete.

- Highlight the cell A1 by pressing the Home key on your keyboard or by pressing the F5 key followed by entering A1.

- Now press the F2.

At this point you will see that the contents of the cell is displayed in such a way the you can alter it. Change the entry 'SALES FIGURES FOR XYZ STORES LTD' to the entry 'SALES FIGURES FOR XYZ STORES PLC' in the manner described.

3.8 Structuring the worksheet

There are several basic editing tools which allow you to make changes to the worksheet in whole or in part.

It is easy to change the appearance of the worksheet by controlling the column width, aligning labels and changing the display format of numbers. Rows and columns can be inserted or deleted and ranges of cells can be erased, copied or moved.

Changing the entire worksheet

It is common to make changes which affect the whole worksheet first. Exceptions can then be dealt with afterwards.

- Chosing from the menu the option Worksheet followed by Global will permit Global changes.

In the example, you can alter all numbers so that they are expressed to two decimal places. Examine screen dump 3.4 to see what you are trying to achieve.

This should show you what is meant by the term 'Global'. Every number is to be expressed to two decimal places.

- From the menu select Worksheet.

- Select Global followed by Format.

You will now be confronted with yet another menu, and many of these options will be discussed later. For now, to choose two decimal places select Fixed and enter the number '2' to indicate this.

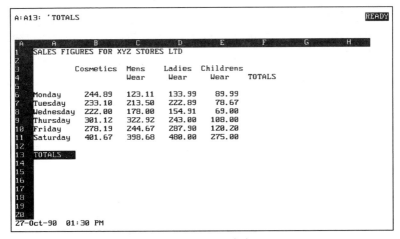

Screen Dump 3.4

You will now see that all numbers on the spreadsheet are expressed as required. In fact, as you will see later, any other numbers added to the spreadsheet will also appear expressed to two decimal places.

Five other basic Global settings are possible:

- Typing Global, Label-Prefix aligns labels after the command is issued. For example Global, Label-Prefix, Right will right Justify text in a range of cells. (Right Justify means moving text to as far right in a cell as it can go.)

- Typing Worksheet, Global, Column-Width sets the column width from 1 to 72 characters wide, the normal setting being 9. You can specify a width by either typing the number of characters or by pointing with left or right cursor keys to narrow or widen the column. Worksheet, Column-Width alters the width of just one column.

- Typing Worksheet, Global, Protection allows or prohibits changes to worksheet entries. When protection is 'on', this can prevent accidental alterations to formulae or data.

- Typing Worksheet, Global, Default allows you to specify the disk and printer settings for the current work session. Settings can be saved for later work if necessary.

- Typing Worksheet, Erase will erase the whole spreadsheet. Be careful using this!

Now return to your spreadsheet.

- Use the Worksheet, Global, Column-Width command to alter all the column widths to 11 characters.

Inserting and deleting rows and columns

- Typing Worksheet, Insert allows you to insert an entire columns or rows and and adjusts the rest of the worksheet accordingly.

- Typing Worksheet, Delete allows you to delete entire columns or rows. For example, to delete column 'D', you would position the cell pointer in column 'D' and select the command sequence type Worksheet, Delete, Column and press Return.

Windows and titles

To view and edit the worksheet efficiently it is useful to keep the most important parts of it in view.

- Typing Worksheet, Windows, Titles freezes headings and titles so that they are shown on screen all the time. For example, the command sequence Worksheet, Windows, Titles, Both freezes the area above and to the left of the pointer.

- Typing Worksheet, Window allows data entry in one part of the spreadsheet whilst being able to see the effects in another.

When using windows you must position the pointer where you want to split the screen.

- Typing Worksheet, Window, Horizontal will keep specified columns in view while Worksheet, Window, Vertical does the same thing for rows.

Only two windows are allowed at a time. To move between windows use key F6.

Normally Windows will scroll together (synchronised). To make just one window move type use the command sequence Worksheet, Window, Unsynchronised.

● Typing /Worksheet, Window, Clear allows you to clear or change window settings in view while Worksheet, Window, Vertical does the same for row totals.

● Use the command sequence /Worksheet, Window, Horizontal with cell pointer at Row 2 in order to keep the days of the week showing. If you find yourself in the wrong window, pressing the F6 will allow you to skip between windows – try it now.

Because you have widened the cells you are unable to see column F. In fact you may even have problems printing the entire spreadsheet because you may not have paper of sufficient width in your printer.

In cell B12 you will place a function that adds the numbers in the range B6..B11. When you do this you will observe that the numbers are still to 2 decimal places and will remain so for all figures until

```
A:B13:  (FZ) @SUM(B6..B11)                                          READY

  A          A          B            C           D           E
 1  SALES FIGURES FOR XYZ STORES LTD
 2
 3             Cosmetics    Mens        Ladies      Childrens
 4                          Wear        Wear        Wear
 5
 6  Monday      244.89      123.11      133.99       89.99
 7  Tuesday     233.10      213.50      222.89       78.67
 8  Wednesday   222.00      178.00      154.91       69.00
 9  Thursday    301.12      322.92      243.00      108.00
10  Friday      278.19      244.67      287.90      120.20
11  Saturday    401.67      398.68      480.00      275.00
12
13  TOTALS      1680.97
14
15
16
17
18
19
20
27-Oct-90   01:36 PM
```

Screen Dump 3.5

otherwise instructed. However the total of 1680.97 might be better displayed as 1,680.97 (i.e. with a comma separating thousands).

3.9 Copying and Moving _____

From the Lotus menu using the command Copy allows you to copy the contents of either one cell or a range of cells from one part of the spreadsheet to another.

Likewise using the command Move from the Lotus menu allows you to move the contents of either one cell or a range of cells from one part of the spreadsheet to another.

In both cases you will be prompted to enter the From and To range.

- Go to cell B13 and enter a function that sums up the cosmetic sales for the week. The entry should be '@SUM(B6..B11)' which sums all values in this range.

- Staying in cell B13, use the /Copy command to copy the formula From B13..B13 To C13..E13.

- Now repeat this process by entering a formula in cell F6 that adds up all the Monday sales and copy this with with its function to the remainder of the days.

When working in column F you will have noticed that column A cannot be seen. If this causes a problem then a vertical window can always be set up that keeps the days in view.

- Now use the Range, Format facility to allow the comma to separate the thousands in both total columns. The format choice will need to be , (Comma) and you will again need to state that output should to be to two decimal places.

When using range formats in this way, it will always override the Global settings previously set. In fact if you were to attempt a Global setting after using range, the range formats would still remain in tact.

Relative, Absolute and Mixed copying _____

Before copying formula, be sure you understand these terms.

Relative records the position of the cell relative to the cell containing the formula. For example, if you copy a formula in B7 which is +B4+B5+B6 to E7 then the resulting formula in E7 will be +E4+E5+E6. The relative position has now moved from B to E and this is reflected in the new formula. If the contents in B7 were moved or copied to F10, then the formula would now be +F7+F8+F9, the letters change to F and the numbers increase by 3.

However, the reference to a specific cell is needed an **absolute** cell address is required. In Lotus this is achieved by using the $ (Dollar) sign. Hence $A$5 indicates a permanent link to the value of column A in Row 5 of the worksheet. In other words, if this appeared in a cell and was copied or moved to any other cell, the formula would stay exactly the same.

It is quite possible to have a mixture of relative and absolute addressing. Hence a **mixed** address $D6 indicates that the column should remain the same with the row changing relatively each time the formula is copied or moved. The formula D$6 would mean that the row remains fixed with the column changing relatively.

- Go to cell A15 and enter the label 'PERCENTAGE OF TOTAL SALES'.

- Now go to Cell B16 and enter the formula '+B13/@SUM($B$13..$E$13)*100'

The effect of this is to divide the cell contents of B13 by the total sales and multiply by 100 to give the percentage. By using the sum range of ($B$13..$E$13) we have set it at the absolute value which remains unchanged when copying. Alternatively, by using B13 as the numerator, it is defined as relative and will change on copying.

- Use the /copy facility to copy From B16..B16 To C16..E16.

- Format the range of percentage values to zero decimal places.

- Examine the formula in each of these cells carefully to gain an understanding of what has happened.

- If you have not already done so, position the cursor in column B and select the command sequence /Worksheet, Window, Vertical to place a window at this place. Use F6 to jump windows and experiment moving around the spreadsheet.

Screen dump 3.6 shows the end result with a vertical window keeping the days in view for ease of reading.

```
A:B16:  +B13/@SUM($B$13..$E$13)×100                              READY

    A       A           B          C          D           E
          SALES FIGURE1  S FOR XYZ STORES LTD
1                     1
2                     2
3                     3  Cosmetics   Mens       Ladies    Childrens
4                     4              Wear       Wear      Wear
5                     5
6         Monday      6  244.89      123.11     133.99     89.99
7         Tuesday     7  233.10      213.50     222.89     78.67
8         Wednesday   8  222.00      178.00     154.91     69.00
9         Thursday    9  301.12      322.92     243.00    108.00
10        Friday     10  278.19      244.67     287.90    120.20
11        Saturday   11  401.67      398.68     480.00    275.00
12                   12
13        TOTALS     13  1,680.97    1,480.88   1,522.69  740.86
14                   14
15        PERCENTAGE O15  F TOTAL SALES
16                   16  30.98       27.30      28.07      13.66
17                   17
18                   18
19                   19
20                   20
27-Oct-90  01:47 PM
```

Screen Dump 3.6

3.10 Saving your work and file handling

- If you have not already done so, save your file.

Remember, the updates you have done on this since you last backed up will not be on disk. File names can be up to eight characters long but cannot include a space. Lotus recognises three types of file and will automatically add a three character extension to each file name entered. They are:

.wk3	for a worksheet file
.prn	for a print file
.pic	for a graph file

When you save a file of data, you do not need to place the full stop and three characters at the end of the file name; the Lotus does this for you. With respect to the graph file, you will work on this in the next chapter.

The purpose of a print file is that rather than print your file direct to the printer, you can place it into a file for printing at a later time.

The file commands are as follows:

● The menu command /File, Save is used to save a file to disk.

● The menu command /File, Retrieve is used to retrieve a file from disk.

● The menu command /File, Combine is used to copy, add or subtract all or part of a worksheet file on disk into the current worksheet at the location of the cell pointer.

● The menu command /File, Xtract is used to extract and save a part of the worksheet in a separate worksheet file.

● The menu command /File, Erase is used to remove one or more files from the disk.

● The menu command /File, List is used to display names of all files of a particular type stored in the current directory and the space, in bytes, still free on the disk.

● The menu command /File, Import is used to import data from programs that have produced standard ASCII files (not for beginners!).

3.12 Manipulating your printer

The final stage in this chapter is to attempt to print the entire spreadsheet. In this exercise you will see how to overcome the problem of your paper not being wide enough for the spreadsheet. This can be achieved either by increasing the right-hand margin to allow more characters per line or reducing the size of print to fit on to standard width paper.

All print commands of this nature can be found in the Print menu.

- Call up the Lotus command menu and select the option Print. As you are going to print direct to the printer, select Printer and make sure your printer is ready.

- You can at this stage select the range to be printed, remembering that you want to print the entire spreadsheet.

When you use print in this way, all the previous settings will remain from the last print. It is important, therefore, that if you have made significant changes to your spreadsheet then you might well need to alter the settings. If, on the other hand, the settings do not need changing, then you can simply select Go at this stage and Lotus will print with the previous settings.

You want to increase the size of the right-hand margin.

- From the menu you are in, select Options.

The Options menu allows you to choose how the spreadsheet is to be printed.

- From here select Margins. Lotus will now ask which margin you want changed. Select Right margin and increase it from its default (usually 76) to 100.

The other margins are for left, top and bottom. If for example, you want your spreadsheet written further down a page then you can set Top to a higher number. Selecting option None clears all margins and reverts back to how it was set up when the Lotus session began.

- If you are a Release 2 user, then from the same options menu select Setup and enter the code '\015'.

This may appear somewhat odd but for most printers it is an ASCII code that reduces the size of print. Do not worry if you do not know about ASCII codes. Another way around this is to select condensed print on your printer. What ever method is used, you might have to consult a printer manual.

- If you are using Release 3, then there is a better way of asking for condensed print. The sequence of commands is /Print, Printer Options, Advanced, Layout, Pitch, Compressed.

- Quit from Options menu and select Go to start the job of printing.

This may seem extremely cumbersome as a way of squeezing a spreadsheet across a piece of paper. There is, however, an alternative to all of this if you are using a later version of Lotus. Rather than printing across the width of paper (called landscape mode) you can print your spreadsheet down the length of the paper (called portrait mode). This can be achieved through the sequence; /Print, Printer, Options, Advanced, Layout, Orientation, Landscape. Such a sequence of commands demonstrates well the nature of the Lotus menu structure

- If you have the Advanced print options, then reset all your margins, cancel out the setup of \015 and print your spreadsheet in landscape as described.

- Finally, change all the numeric values (not the formulae) to make certain that the spreadsheet is actually doing the job it is supposed to.

It can be extremely useful not simply to print a spreadsheet in the form we want it presented, but to print all the actual contents of the cells, especially the formulae, to help see what the spreadsheet is actually doing. The command sequence for this is /Print, Printer, Options, Other, Cell-formulae. Attempt this now but remember to change it back to 'as-displayed' before printing using the sequence /Print, Printer, Options, Other, As-displayed.

3.13 Summary _____

This chapter has concentrated on how the Lotus commands are organised in a hierarchical menu structure. You will have probably begun to appreciate that the command structure is large and not always straightforward regarding what sequence of commands should be used to achieve certain objectives. Finding your way around menus will become easier through practice and experience.

With respect to both file handling and printing, we have examined only a part of what can be achieved. However, in both cases you have seen the important principles involved.

In this chapter you have:

- Understood the idea of Lotus multi-level menu structure of commands

- Understood the idea of a command sequence

- Saved a file and retrieved it

- Used a tree diagram to gain a better overview of the menu structure

- Printed a spreadsheet

- Edited text

- Restructured a spreadsheet using both /Worksheet, Global as well as /Range

- Set up a window

- Set up and copied cell formulae with relative, absolute and mixed addressing

- Examined the differing file types

- Altered the appearance of printed spreadsheets

4 SOME STATISTICS AND A FIRST GRAPH

4.1 Aims of this chapter

Lotus has an extremely useful graphing facility that is able to put a much finer touch to your data. The purpose of this chapter, therefore, is to help you get familiar with this as well as to develop your spreadsheet skills further.

Apart from being able to draw graphs, you will see that once the graph has been set up, it is instantly redrawn as the data changes. Later in the book, chapter 8 will take graphs to a more advanced stage.

4.2 Entering the statistics

• Get into your spreadsheet in preparation for entering the required information into the spreadsheet. Look at screen dump 4.1 to see what you will be aiming at for the first exercise in this chapter.

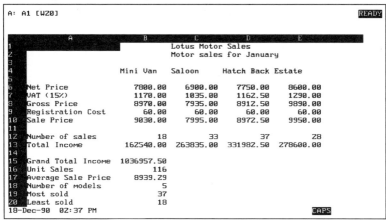

A: A1 [W20]				READY
A	B	C	D	E
1		Lotus Motor Sales		
2		Motor sales for January		
3				
4	Mini Van	Saloon	Hatch Back	Estate
5				
6 Net Price	7800.00	6900.00	7750.00	8600.00
7 VAT (15%)	1170.00	1035.00	1162.50	1290.00
8 Gross Price	8970.00	7935.00	8912.50	9890.00
9 Registration Cost	60.00	60.00	60.00	60.00
10 Sale Price	9030.00	7995.00	8972.50	9950.00
11				
12 Number of sales	18	33	37	28
13 Total Income	162540.00	263835.00	331982.50	278600.00
14				
15 Grand Total Income	1036957.50			
16 Unit Sales	116			
17 Average Sale Price	8939.29			
18 Number of models	5			
19 Most sold	37			
20 Least sold	18			
18-Dec-90 02:37 PM				CAPS

Screen Dump 4.1

Think about how you are going to layout the information, in particular which of the figures are calculated by Lotus.

- Move the cursor to cell C1 and type 'Lotus Motor Sales'. Then press ENTER to enter the label into the spreadsheet. (Do this after each cell entry.)

- Move to cell C2 and enter 'Motor sales for January 1991'.

When entering labels to the spreadsheet, the use of the Backspace key allows you to delete characters while entering text. Also, if text is already on the spreadsheet, you can edit an entry by using F2.

- Commence with the following entries:

In cell	Type	Press
B4	Mini Van	Right Arrow
C4	Saloon	Right Arrow
D4	Hatch Back	Right Arrow
E4	Estate	Right Arrow
F4	Truck	ENTER

You will find that the labels are a little too tight, so you will need to widen the columns. It would be wise to widen all columns to 10.

- Use the command sequence, /Worksheet, Global, Column-Set and enter 10.

- Press F5 (the Goto key) and type 'A6'. From this proceed with the following entries:

In cell	type	Press
A6	Net Price	Down Arrow
A7	VAT (15%)	Down Arrow
A8	Gross Price	Down Arrow
A9	Registration Cost	Down Arrow
A10	Sale Price	Down Arrow (TWICE)
A12	Number of sales	Down Arrow
A13	Total Income	Down Arrow (TWICE)
A15	Grand Total Income	Down Arrow

A16	Unit Sales	Down Arrow
A17	Average Sale Price	Down Arrow
A18	Number of models	Down Arrow
A19	Most sold	Down Arrow
A20	Least sold	Down Arrow

Having entered all of this, it should become apparent that column A is a bit tight if you are to enter figures in column B. You will now widen the column.

● Press '/' to call up the commands.

● Enter the following sequence (point to or press the first letter of each) Worksheet, Column, Set-Width.

● Use the Right Arrow key to widen the column. A width of 20 will do.

● Press F5 and move to cell B6.

● Enter the basic prices of the cars as whole numbers in cells B6 to F6. See screen dump 4.1 for details.

Now change all the figures to two places of decimal so that you can deal in money.

● Enter the command sequence Worksheet, Global, Format, Fixed and press ENTER to accept the default value of 2 decimal places.

● Press F5 and go to B7 and enter the formula '+B6*0.15' to create a value of 15% for VAT.

You now need to copy the formula in B7 across the spreadsheet. You should do this by pointing to cells rather than entering cell ranges.

● Press '/C' to use the Copy command. Now Press ENTER.

The panel should now show the words 'ENTER range to copy FROM B7..B7'.

● Press ENTER to accept this.

The Copy To range now appears.

● Move to the start of the target range by pressing the Right Arrow key so that you are in cell C7. Anchor this cell by pressing '.' (full stop). Now press the Right Arrow key again three times to highlight the area that you want to copy to. Having done this press ENTER.

The VAT should appear. Move the cursor along to Row 7 and look at the formula in the top left of the display screen. What do you notice? At this point it might be worth referring to the explanation given in the previous chapter between relative and absolute cell values. In this case, you will see what effect copying formulae has on relative cell values.

● Move to cell B8 and enter '+B6+B7' and copy this formula across the table (you should know how to do this by now). Try to type the ranges this time rather than pointing to them.

● Enter '60' into B9 and copy that too across the table.

● In B10 enter '+B8+B9' and copy this formula into the cell range C10..F10.

The top part of your spreadsheet should now be complete.

● Enter the monthly sales figures in B12 through to F12 as shown in screen dump 4.1. You will have to enter these numbers.

You now have car sales expressed to 2 decimal places. You need a range command in order to express these figures as whole numbers.

● Use the command sequence Range, Format, Fixed and type 0 for the number of decimal places. Press ENTER to reveal the message 'ENTER Range to format'.

● Type (or point) 'B12..F12' and press ENTER.

Your range of figures should now be whole numbers.

● In B13 you enter the formula '+B10*B12' and Copy this formula across the row.

In B15 you need to enter the sum of the values from B13 to F13. It is quite legitimate to type '+B13+C13+...' and so on. The problem with adding up rows or columns of figures in this way is that it will take too long to construct the formula. A quicker way is to use one of the 123 functions which is prefixed with a '@' symbol.

● Enter '@SUM(B13..F13)' in cell B15.

What you will get is a row of asterisks. Don't worry; Lotus is telling you that it has a figure that will not quite fit into the cell, so widen the column in the same way as shown earlier; eleven characters wide should do.

In cell A16 much the same principle is required to add up the unit sales in the range B12..F12.

● Enter '@SUM(B12..F12)' in cell B16.

This time the column cells are wide enough to take the number.

Cell B17 is to contain the average price of a unit sale. This will be found by dividing the total units sold by the grand total income which would take the form '+B15/@SUM(B12..F12)'. Alternatively, the total number of units sold has already been worked out for cell B16, so the formulae is '+B15/B16'.

● In B17 type '+B15/@SUM(B12..F12)'.

● In B18 type '@COUNT(B4..F4)'. This should give you the 5 types of differing models sold. Reformat the cell to show a whole figure.

The function @COUNT works out the number of cells that have data in them. Other functions will be useful to determine the model that sold the most (@MAX) and the ones that sold the least (@MIN).

● In B19 type '@MAX(B12..F12)'. This should pick up the most models sold Row 12. Similarly entering '@MIN(B12..F12)' in B25 should give you the least sold Row 12.

Obviously these functions are of more use when you have lots more figures to search through, but this exercise shows the point.

- Now save this worksheet with the command sequence File, Save and enter a file name, such as 'motors'.

- Print the spreadsheet using the command sequence of Print, Printer, Range. Then type or point to the range 'A1..F20'. Check the paper in your printer and then enter Go.

If you are a Release 2 user, then proceed with the next section. To avoid any repetition of graph production, a number of graphs have been placed at the end of this chapter. Your attention will be drawn to them on a number of occasions. If you are a Release 3 user then skip to the section 'Producing a graph with RELEASE 3'.

4.3   Producing a graph with RELEASE 2

- Enter the command /Graph followed by Type and then Bar. At this point we have selected the Graphs command and selected a Bar Chart as the type of graph required.

Screen Dump 4.2 shows the Graphs menu that appears. The highlighted option Type allows you to select a number of ways in which your data can be presented in graph form. When this is selected a number of choices of graph are offered. For the purpose of this chapter, you will work with a Bar chart because this is the easiest to begin with.

- Select 'A' for the first data range. Because you are going to plot only the total sales value for the graph, you only need the one data range. To select the range to be plotted, enter or point to cell range 'B13..F13'.

The purpose of this is to decide what the Bars should represent. In this case, you are saying that you want five bars for each category of vehicle. When selecting 'A', you are determining what the first set of Bars are representing. In a later chapter in the book you will investigate the idea of using more than one set. You will observe that there are a possible six sets of Bars from A to F.

- Select View to examine what has been achieved so far.

```
A: A1 [W20]                                                          MENU
Type  X  A  B  C  D  E  F  Reset  View  Save  Options  Name  Group  Quit
Set graph type
          A              B         C         D         E
1                              Lotus Motor Sales
2                              Motor sales for January
3
4                         Mini Van  Saloon   Hatch Back Estate
5
6    Net Price            7800.00   6900.00   7750.00   8600.00
7    VAT (15%)            1170.00   1035.00   1162.50   1290.00
8    Gross Price          8970.00   7935.00   8912.50   9890.00
9    Registration Cost      60.00     60.00     60.00     60.00
10   Sale Price           9030.00   7995.00   8972.50   9950.00
11
12   Number of sales          18        33        37        28
13   Total Income        162540.00 263835.00 331982.50 278600.00
14
15   Grand Total Income  1036957.50
16   Unit Sales               116
17   Average Sale Price   8939.29
18   Number of models         5
19   Most sold                37
20   Least sold               18
18-Dec-90  02:38 PM
```

Screen Dump 4.2

● Select ESC to return to the Graphs menu.

Graph 4.1 is an example of what you should have achieved. If you have not managed to get this graph, then return to the start of this

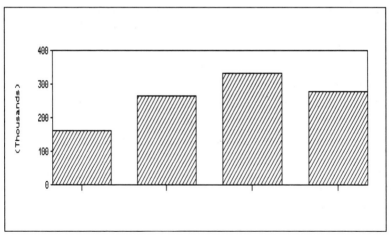

Graph 4.1

section and enter the commands again. Each bar in the chart now represents the sales value of each type of vehicle; the higher the bar the greater the sales value.

Although the graph is technically sound, you need to add a few labels and features to give it some meaning. The graph has no title telling you what it represents, the axes are not labelled and there is no way of seeing what model of car is represented by each bar.

● From the Graph menu select the sequence of commands Options, Titles, First and type in the first line of your graphs title, 'Lotus Motor Sales'.

Now have a quick look at your graph to see the effect. You can now print a second title line.

● From the Graph, Options menu enter the sequence of commands Titles, Second and type in the second line of your graphs title, 'Sales types by value'.

Again view the graph to see the effect. We now need to label both the X and Y axes.

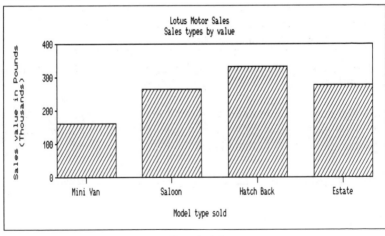

Graph 4.2

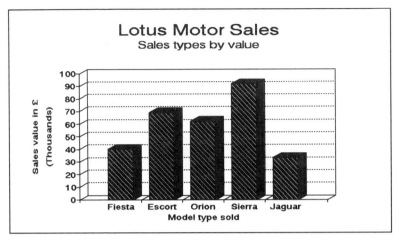

Graph 4.3

- From the Graph, Options menu enter the commands sequence Titles, X-axis 'Model type sold'. Repeat this for the Y-axis with the title 'Sales value in pounds'.

Graph 4.2 reveals that the axes have been labelled with titles as required. All we need to do now is to label each of the five bar points on the X-axis with the vehicle types.

- From the Graph menu select 'X' and type or point to the range which covers the five vehicle types 'B4..F4'.

View the graph again in order to check your work. You will note that the Graph menu option 'X' is used to label each of your Bars. Graph 4.3 shows the result you should now have.

4.4 Printing the graph

The stages to printing a graph

There are a number of stages required when printing a graph which are illustrated in the diagram overleaf:

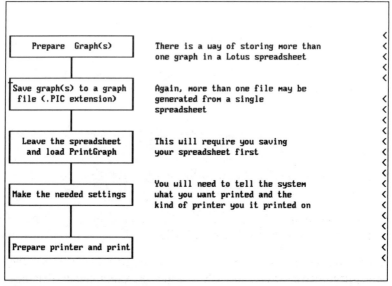

Prepare Graph(s)	There is a way of storing more than one graph in a Lotus spreadsheet
Save graph(s) to a graph file (.PIC extension)	Again, more than one file may be generated from a single spreadsheet
Leave the spreadsheet and load PrintGraph	This will require you saving your spreadsheet first
Make the needed settings	You will need to tell the system what you want printed and the kind of printer you it printed on
Prepare printer and print	

Working with multiple graphs

Most of this chapter so far has concentrated on the preparation stage of a graph. However, you have not examined the idea of working with more than one graph. In order to avoid any confusion with disk files, Lotus talks about naming graphs as opposed to saving graphs.

● From the Graph menu call up Name.

The only two options you need to worry about for now are the Create and Use options.

● Select Create and then in response to Lotus asking you what you want to call your graph, enter 'Bars'.

At this point, you will have created a graph that is part of your spreadsheet. If you wish, you can now create a completely different graph and create a distinct name for that one as well. By doing this you can create a whole series of graphs for later use.

The Use option then allows you to recall a previously named graph rather than have to start again setting up all the parameters.

Saving your graph

This is quite different to the previous option. In order to print a graph, Lotus Release 2 has a separate program called PrintGraph that requires a file separate from the spreadsheet. To achieve this you will need to save the graph from the spreadsheet into a graph file that has a '.PIC' extension to it. Such file extensions were discussed in chapter 1.

Before starting, save the spreadsheet as a precaution against anything going wrong.

● Return to the main 123 menu by pressing the ESC key until it appears at the top of your screen.

● Enter the command sequence /File, Save and accept the file name that appears simply by pressing ENTER.

The file has been saved in place of the version previously saved. The only difference between this file and the previous one is that this spreadsheet has a graph attached to it. It is possible to have more than one graph attached to a spreadsheet. To do this, you will need to save graphs under their own name.

● From the spreadsheet enter the command sequence /Graph, Save and enter a graph name; e.g. 'sales'. This will now store the graph on disk with the name 'sales.pic'.

● Return to the main 123 menu and leave the spreadsheet altogether by entering the command /Quit.

You will find yourself out of 123 and should select the option PrintGraph to be ready to print the graph.

PrintGraph lists all files that can be printed; i.e. all files that end with '.PIC'. As only one file exists, this should now be highlighted. Examine screen dump 4.3 before progressing to make sure that your PrintGraph program has been set up.

If your PrintGraph has been set up then the panel should reveal the following:

```
Copyright 1986 Lotus Development Corp.  All Rights Reserved. Release 2.01  MENU

Select graphs for printing
Image-Select  Settings  Go  Align  Page  Exit

   GRAPH      IMAGE OPTIONS                    HARDWARE SETUP
   IMAGES      Size           Range Colors      Graphs Directory:
   SELECTED    Top       .395  X Black           C:\123
   sales       Left      .750  A Black          Fonts Directory:
               Width    6.500  B Black           C:\123
               Height   4.691  C Black          Interface:
               Rotate    .000  D Black           Parallel 1
                               E Black          Printer Type:
               Font            F Black           IBM GP,Pro/hi
               1  BLOCK1                        Paper Size
               2  BLOCK1                         Width     8.500
                                                 Length   11.000

                                                ACTION OPTIONS
                                                Pause: No   Eject: No
```

Screen Dump 4.3

- Graphs directory should show where the graphs are kept. If you installed the software as suggested then this should be in C:\123.

- Fonts directory should also be in C:\123 if you followed the installation advice in this book. Fonts are where the printer information is kept.

A printer type should be installed showing what printer is being used.

If for some reason file names are not appearing on the screen, then your PrintGraph program will need to be configured. To select the required graph begin by selecting the Image-Select option and then highlight the Bars graph and press ENTER. Your chosen graph image will have the # (hash) symbol beside it indicating that this has been selected. Screen dump 4.4 shows the kind of screen that should appear when selecting an image.

If you do not need to configure PrintGraph then jump to the next section.

Configuring PrintGraph

You must first set up the printer.

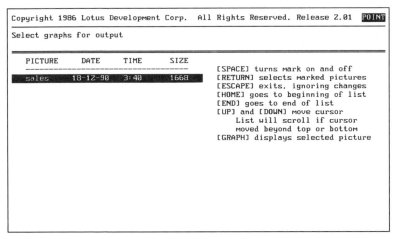

```
Copyright 1986 Lotus Development Corp.  All Rights Reserved. Release 2.01  POINT

Select graphs for output


  PICTURE      DATE     TIME     SIZE
  ------------------------------------        [SPACE] turns mark on and off
   sales     18-12-90   3:40     1668         [RETURN] selects marked pictures
                                              [ESCAPE] exits, ignoring changes
                                              [HOME] goes to beginning of list
                                              [END] goes to end of list
                                              [UP] and [DOWN] move cursor
                                                 List will scroll if cursor
                                                 moved beyond top or bottom
                                              [GRAPH] displays selected picture
```

Screen Dump 4.4

- Select from the main PrintGraph menu the Settings option and from there the Printer option.

- You should now have a list of printers available like that shown in screen dump 4.5. Highlight the one required (usually the high density one) and press the space key to indicate this is the one you want. The '#' sign should appear next to the chosen option.

- Press ESC until you return to the main PrintGraph menu.

The next step is to set up the graphs directory.

- Select from the main PrintGraph menu the Settings option and from there the Graphs-Directory.

- You now need to state where the graph files with the .pic extension are being held. Screen dump 4.5 illustrates what is required.

- Press 'ESC' until you return to the main PrintGraph menu.

Screen dump 4.6 shows a setting where the directory set up is on A: (usually a floppy disk) while what is wanted is directory C:\123.

Now you must to set up the fonts directory.

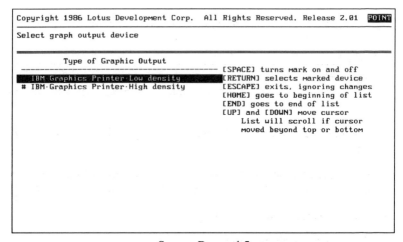

Screen Dump 4.5

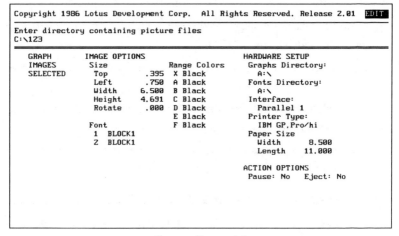

Screen Dump 4.6

- Select from the main PrintGraph menu the Settings option and from there the Fonts-Directory.

- You now need to state where the font files are being held.

● Press ESC until you return to the main PrintGraph menu.

Printing

● Make sure you are at the main PrintGraph menu with Image-Select highlighted as shown in screen dump 4.4. Press ENTER at this stage.

You should have a list of graph files with the .pic file extension being displayed.

● Press the space bar. A '#' sign will appear in front of the file name to indicate that this is the file selected for printing. Press ENTER.

● Adjust the paper and select Align.

● Select Go to begin printing.

● When printing is finished, select Page to advance the paper.

● From the main PrintGraph menu, select the Exit option to return to the main Lotus opening screen.

● Call up the Lotus 123 spreadsheet (worksheet) if you intend to progress through this chapter.

● Now recall your worksheet file using the command sequence /File, Retrieve and sales to load the file into memory.

As you are a Release 2 user there is no need to work on the next section. Skip to section 4.6, Trying other graphs.

4.5 Producing a graph with RELEASE 3 _____

With respect to graphs, two of the main differences offered by Release 3 compared with Release 2 are the facility for printing a graph without leaving the spreadsheet and being able to view a graph while at the same time being able to work with the spreadsheet.

● Enter the command sequence /Graph, Type, Bar. You have now selected the Graphs command and selected a Bar chart as the type graph required.

```
A: A1: [W20]                                                          MENU
Type  X  A  B  C  D  E  F  Reset  View  Save  Options  Name  Group  Quit
Set graph type
            A              B         C          D            E
1                               Lotus Motor Sales
2                               Motor sales for January
3
4                        Mini Van    Saloon    Hatch Back Estate
5
6    Net Price              7800.00   6900.00    7750.00     8600.00
7    VAT (15%)              1170.00   1035.00    1162.50     1290.00
8    Gross Price            8970.00   7935.00    8912.50     9890.00
9    Registration Cost        60.00     60.00      60.00       60.00
10   Sale Price             9030.00   7995.00    8972.50     9950.00
11
12   Number of sales             18        33         37          28
13   Total Income        162540.00 263835.00  331982.50   278600.00
14
15   Grand Total Income 1036957.50
16   Unit Sales                116
17   Average Sale Price     8939.29
18   Number of models            5
19   Most sold                  37
20   Least sold                 18
18-Dec-90  02:54 PM
```

Screen Dump 4.7

Screen dump 4.7 shows the Graphs menu that appears. The highlighted option Type allows you to select a number of ways in which your data can be presented in graph form. When this is selected a number of choices of graph are offered. For the purpose of this chapter, you will work with a Bar chart because this is the easiest to begin with.

- Select 'A' for the first data range. As we are going to plot only the total income for the graph, we only need the one data range. To select the range to be plotted, enter or point to cell range 'B13..F13'.

The purpose of this is to decide what the Bars should represent. In this case, you are saying that we want five Bars for each category of vehicle. When selecting 'A' you are determining what the first set of Bars are representing. In a later chapter in the book you will investigate the idea of using more than one set. You will observe that there are a possible six sets of Bars from A to F.

- Select View to examine what has been achieved so far.

- Select ESC to return to the Graphs menu.

Graph 4.1 is an example of what you should have achieved. If you have not managed to get this graph, then return to the start of this section and enter the commands again. Each Bar in the chart now represents the sales value of each model of car; the higher the Bar the greater the sales value.

Although the graph is technically sound, you need to add a few labels and features to give it some meaning. The graph has no title telling you what it represents, the axes are not labelled and there is no way of seeing what model of vehicle is represented by each Bar.

● From the Graph menu select the sequence of commands Options, Titles, First and type in the first line of your graphs title, 'Lotus Motor Sales'.

Now have a quick look at your graph to see the effect. You can now print a second title line.

● From the Graph, Options menu enter the sequence of commands Titles, Second and type in the second line of your graphs title, 'Sales types by value'.

Again view the graph to see the effect. We now need to label both the X and Y axes.

● From the Graph, Options menu enter the commands sequence Titles, X-axis 'Model type sold'. Repeat this for the Y-axis with the title 'Sales value in pounds'.

Graph 4.2 reveals the axes have been labelled with titles as required. All we need to do now is to label each of the five bar points on the X-axis with the vehicle types.

● From the Graph menu select 'X' and type or point to the range which covers the five vehicle types 'B4..F4'.

View the graph again in order to check your work. You will note that the Graph menu option 'X' is used to label each of your Bars. Graph 4.3 shows the result you should now have.

Working with multiple graphs

Most of this chapter so far has concentrated on the preparation stage of a graph. However, you have not examined the idea of working with more than one graph. The principle is that you can store into memory an existing graph while working on another one. In fact, you can store many graphs all as part of the same spreadsheet. Indeed, as a Release 3 user you can also work on more than one spreadsheet at any given time.

● From the Graph menu call up Name. This should reveal the kind of menu shown in screen dump 4.8.

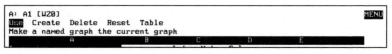

Screen Dump 4.8

The only two options you need to worry about for now are the Create and Use options.

● Select Create and then in response to Lotus asking you what you want to call your graph, enter 'Bars'.

At this point, you will have created a graph that is part of your spreadsheet. If you wish, you can now create a completely different graph and create a distinct name for that one as well. By doing this you can create a whole series of graphs for later use.

The Use Option then allows you to recall a previously named graph rather than have to start again setting up all the parameters.

Saving and printing your graph

Printing a graph in Lotus Release 3 is rather like printing a spreadsheet.

● Make sure you have the main menu showing and select the Print menu from this.

● As with spreadsheet printing, you should select the Printer to instruct you want output to your printer.

At this point it is worth making sure that your printer is on and there is paper in it.

● Now select Image followed by Current.

This means that you want a graph to be printed which to Lotus is an image stored in memory. By selecting Current, you are going to print the current graph that has been worked on. If you selected Named-Graph as opposed Current graph, then you would have been given a list of named graphs to choose from.

● Now select Go to start the printing.

Printing a graph is quite a sophisticated job for any computer as an image has to be built up in the computer's memory so that it knows what each line should be. Consequently, this may be a slow process depending on the kind of printer you have.

Window your graph

Release 3 has benefit of allowing you to see both your spreadsheet and graph together. In doing this you will see the graph display on the right side of the screen with the spreadsheet displayed on the left. You can use column E as the dividing point.

● Position your cursor at column E.

● From the main Lotus menu, select Worksheet and then Window.

● Now select Graph.

You will observe that you can still work with your spreadsheet while viewing the Bar chart at the same time.

● Alter the value of monthly sales of Estates 28 to 33 and observe how the graph changes instantly in the window.

4.6 Trying other graphs

As a final exercise, it is now worth experimenting with other types of graphs. For example, you might wish to see the distribution of vehicle types sold to be seen as a pie chart, giving some perspective what sells most and least.

- From the /Graph menu, select the Type option and select the Pie chart. Now use the view option to see the effect.

The pie chart in screen dump 4.9 shows the result. You will notice that not all of the information in the bar chart was needed by the pie chart. In particular, the Y-Axis title is not used because the pie chart has no use for it.

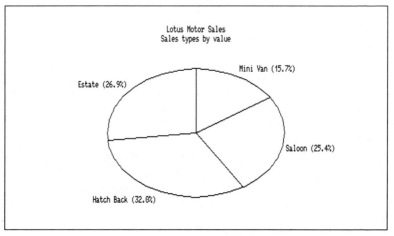

Screen Dump 4.9

Many of the types of graph that are available are not well suited to this kind of example. However, there is no harm in experimenting with some of the other types of graph.

4.7 Some final points

During the work covered in this chapter and the previous chapter you have been taken through some sophisticated steps that now need some more explanation.

At the left-hand end of the first line on the screen, Lotus displays all the information about the current cell. First its address, then (in brackets) its display format (decimal places, currency, etc.) and finally its contents.

At the right-hand end of the first line is a mode indicator. You should keep an eye on this field because it tells you what 123 is doing or wants you to do. Here are a few of the common indications:

Indicator	Mode
READY	Waiting for you to enter a command or make a cell entry
VALUE	A number or formula is being entered
LABEL	A label is being entered
EDIT	A cell entry is being entered
POINT	A range is being pointed to
MENU	A menu item is being selected
HELP	A help screen is in use
ERROR	An error has occurred and 123 is waiting for you to press the ESC or Return key to acknowledge
WAIT	Calculating is in progress and the computer cannot take further instructions

When an error has occurred, 123 displays a message about it in the bottom left-hand corner of the screen. To get back to the READY mode you must hit ESC or Return.

123's main job is to do arithmetic for us and, because certain types of computation keep recurring, it has been provided with a set of formulae to do these computations. These built-in formulae are called functions. You have used the SUM function already and the others are used in much the same way.

A function reference, say @SUM(B6..D10), comprises three elements:

1 An @ which distinguishes its entry from a label

2 The function name, SUM

3 Data or the range containing the data to be used

The information in brackets is often called the argument or the parameters of the function. @SUM(B6..D10) simply means sum all the numbers contained in the rectangular range of cells with corners B6 and D10.

Lotus 123 provides far more functions than a set of notes like this can begin to mention. However, here are few of the key ones that you will most likely want to use:

@SUM(range)	Sum of the numeric cells in the range
@COUNT(range)	Number of non-blank cells in the range
@MAX(range)	Maximum value in the range
@MIN(range)	Minimum value in the range
@AVG(range)	Average of non-blank cells in the range

4.8 Chapter Summary

In this chapter, you have:

- Covered more work on text, numeric, formula and function entries to cells

- Altered column widths and formats

- Covered more on using the Copy facility

- Set up a graph

- Named and printed a graph

- Experimented with different types of graph

5 STYLE AND PRESENTATION

5.1 Aims of this chapter

This chapter will show you how to present your spreadsheet in a form that is appropriate to the problem in hand. For example, if your spreadsheet is designed to set out in table form the stock movements for a manufacturing company, then stock values should be stated in whole figures, while stock values should be expressed in a currency value and (possibly) to two decimal places.

Likewise, if a cell in your spreadsheet is to show a date, then it needs to be formatted in the appropriate way. Some time will be spent in this chapter explaining the way Lotus can manipulate dates and perform some very useful date calculations with the next chapter applying the principles yet further.

5.2 Starting off

As a starting point you will examine some styles of presentation using the example set out in screen dump 5.1

Set this spreadsheet up observing that has been no attempt to format any of the cell entries. You will find that the width of cells will need to be adjusted in order to allow some of the long titles to be inserted. In this example cells A and B have been widened to 13 and 22 respectively.

A way around widening cells is to miss out certain columns when entering data into cells. This means that some columns would need to be left empty. In most cases you should avoid this practice because it can lead to confusion later on. By widening cells in this way it is quite clear that a column of data has not been left out.

Altering cell widths can be achieved by moving the cursor into a cell in the column for which you want to widen and then choosing the

```
A:D19:                                                            MENU
Worksheet  Range  Copy  Move  File  Print  Graph  Data  System  Quit
Global, Insert, Delete, Column, Erase, Titles, Window, Status, Page, Hide
   A         A              B              C       D        E       F
1    Gardening equipment stock list
2
3    Stock code    Description         Number   Sell Price
4
5    LM 233        Lawn Mower Delux       12     135.67
6    LM 236        Lawn Mower Standard    11      68.7
7    LM 240        Strimmer Super          9      23.78
8    LM 244        Hand Mower Set          7        40
9    HC 101        Hedge Cutter            9      73.6
10   GH 21         Garden Hose 30m        17      14.99
11   GH 23         Garden Hose 50m        13        20
12   TL 100        Digging Tool           18        14
13   TL 105        Digging Spade          11      14.87
14   TL 110        Lawn Shears            13      16.01
15   TL 115        Border Fork            16      16.5
16   TL 120        Hand Shears             9      19.56
17   TL 125        Pruning Knife          13      12.5
18   WB 100        Wheelbarrow             5      28.56
19
20
27-Oct-90   05:14 PM
```

Screen Dump 5.1

options Worksheet, Column, Set-Width. Then enter the column width
number or press the Right Arrow key to get the desired width.

The numbers that were entered to the spreadsheet have been given an
assumed format. Any number entered that has no decimal value will
always be assumed as a whole number and presented as such. In the
case of the column holding money values, some are set to no decimal
places (integer) while others to one and two. It would seem obvious
that as this represents money, it should be shown as pounds and pence
with two decimal places.

5.3 Defining and using a range

On the way to achieving this, it is worth explaining some concepts, a
few of which you have already met. The first thing to identify is what
range has to formatted. A range is a rectangle of cells as small as one
cell or as large as the whole spreadsheet, for example, A1..M36,
B4..B9. In this case you want to format the range 'D5..D18' to two
decimal places.

Call up Range from your menu. You should observe at the top of your
screen the text shown in screen dump 5.2.

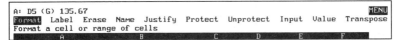

Screen Dump 5.2

The format option, because it is the first of the options in the Range list, is already highlighted. Some of the others are examined later in the chapter. For now simply press ENTER on the format option because it is the formatting of a range that you want.

Now you will see what is shown in screen dump 5.3.

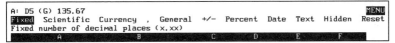

Screen Dump 5.3

At this stage, there are two possibilities of achieving what is wanted. The Currency option will allow you to format a range of cells prefixed with a currency symbol while the Fixed option simply sets a range to a specified number of decimal places. For now, opt for Currency.

● Select Currency either by typing C or using the cursor to highlight the option and pressing ENTER.

● You will be asked how many decimal places it is to be set to. Lotus assumes 2 being most likely and suggests this number. Press ENTER to indicate that this is what you want.

Now it is time to select the required range. Use the method of pointing for defining a range.

● If the cursor is already pointing at one corner of the range, just use the arrow keys to highlight the area. If not, hit the ESC key, move the cursor to a corner of the range (cell D5), and press the '.' (full stop) to anchor it. Then move the cursor to the end of the range (cell D18) highlighting what has to be formatted. When you press ENTER you should see the kind of spreadsheet showing in screen dump 5.2.

```
A: D5 (C2) 135.67                                                    READY

        A               B                C       D         E       F
1   Gardening equipment stock list
2
3   Stock code    Description        Number    Sell Price
4
5   LM 233        Lawn Mower Delux       12    $135.67
6   LM 236        Lawn Mower Standard    11    $68.70
7   LM 240        Strimmer Super          9    $23.78
8   LM 244        Hand Mower Set          7    $40.00
9   HC 101        Hedge Cutter            9    $73.60
10  GH 21         Garden Hose 30m        17    $14.99
11  GH 23         Garden Hose 50m        13    $20.00
12  TL 100        Digging Tool           18    $14.00
13  TL 105        Digging Spade          11    $14.87
14  TL 110        Lawn Shears            13    $16.01
15  TL 115        Border Fork            16    $16.50
16  TL 120        Hand Shears             9    $19.56
17  TL 125        Pruning Knife          13    $12.50
18  WB 100        Wheelbarrow             5    $28.56
19
20
18-Dec-90   10:10 PM
```

Screen Dump 5.4

As you can see the currency sign shows $. If this is not as required then repeat the stages of formatting the cells but use the Fixed option and set the range of numbers to 2 decimal places.

5.4 Copying a range

You will now examine a further use of the range idea by seeing how you can speed up formula replication (copying).

● Set up a column heading called 'Stock Value' in cell E3. You will have to widen column D to avoid clashing with the heading titles.

A formula is a mathematical expression beginning with a '+' sign, for example; +C3/(B5*D2), +D6*@SUM(F6..D9). In this example you want to place into cell E5 the Number of Stock (cell C5) multiplied by the Selling Price (cell D5).

● Move to cell E5 and enter the formula '+C5*D5'.

You will now copy this formula from cell E5 to E6 through to E18. In fact what you will do is to COPY RANGE E5..E5 TO RANGE E6..E18.

- Staying in cell E5, call the menu command in Lotus Copy.

- You are now being asked which range you want to COPY FROM. As your cursor is located in cell E5, Lotus is suggesting the range E5..E5. Press ENTER to accept this suggestion.

- You are now being asked which cell to COPY TO. Move the cursor to cell E6, which is the starting point of the range. Use the full stop to anchor the cursor and then move the cursor to cell E18. The range will then be highlighted. Press ENTER to complete the process.

At this point, the numeric columns should appear like this:

Number	Sell Price	Stock Value
12	135.67	1628.04
11	68.70	755.7
9	23.78	214.02
7	40.00	280
9	73.60	662.4
17	14.99	254.83
13	20.00	260
18	14.00	252
11	14.87	163.57
13	16.01	208.13
16	16.50	264
9	19.56	176.04
13	12.50	162.5
5	28.56	142.8

5.5 More on formats

The problem you are left with is that the Value column has the wrong format. On this occasion, try a slightly different format.

- Use the command sequence /Range, Format , (comma) and press ENTER to accept the suggestion of format to 2 decimal places. Then enter the range to format as E5..E18.

The effect of this command is to insert commas in the longer numbers to help make them become more readable.

Commands may be selected by moving the cursor to highlight a required command and pressing Return; a useful facility if you are not sure of yourself because the third line from the top of the screen gives an indication of what the highlighted command will do. Alternatively you can achieve it by pressing the initial letter of a command on the menu line.

In summary, the following options are available for either Range formats or Global formats:

FIXED   Sets a number display to a specific number of decimal places

SCIENTIFIC   Number is set to the form 4.732E-2

CURRENCY   Commas are used to separate thousands, the numbers with a dollar sign in front of them and negative numbers placed in brackets

COMMA ,   Commas are used to separate thousands

GENERAL   The default format; number normally as input but insignificant zeros to right of decimal point are suppressed

PERCENT   Multiplies stored values by 100 and places a % sign at the end of them

DATE   Treats the number as a date value, see later

TEXT ,   Displays the formula underlying the number normally shown. This can come in handy when you want to see more technically what you have done

The same can be arrived at when using Worksheet, Global, Format. In this instance, the entire spreadsheet will be set to the specified format unless otherwise set by a Range, Format.

5.6 Presenting text

When text is preceded by ' it will be left justified. When it is preceded by " it will be right justified in a cell. If it is preceded by ^, then the text will be centred in the cell. Text entries starting with a number or a mathematical symbol will have to be preceded by one of these text labels if it is not to be treated as a value or formula entry.

If you have already entered your text and you subsequently want it altered, Lotus offers a way of achieving this without you having to key in every text cell again.

● Go to cell B5 and call the Lotus menu of commands.

● From this menu select the command sequence Range, Label and observe the menu that says Center, Right or Left.

You are going to change the range B5..B18 from being left justified to right justified.

● Call the Right option and state the range 'B5..B18'.

You may not like this. If you don't change it back to left justified. The effect of this is to change all the text from preceding with ' to the " without any entry of new data. Experiment by setting the heading title on Row 3 to centre.

5.7 Inserts, deletions and erasures

You will now add two new extra columns, one column called 'Minimum' and the other 'shortfall'. The Minimum column will hold the minimum stock that the business should hold of this item. The next column will hold the shortfall if the actual number is less than this minimum.

● First insert a column by placing your cursor anywhere in Row D and selecting the Lotus command sequence Worksheet, Insert, Column.

Lotus is now asking where you want the column inserted and is suggesting it should be at the current column.

- Press ENTER to insert a new blank column in this location.

From inspection, you should note that the formulae have been adjusted to reflect the newly structured spreadsheet.

Some of the other Inserts, Deletes and Erasures are:

Worksheet, Insert, Row	Inserts one or more rows
Worksheet, Delete, Row	Deletes one or more rows
Worksheet, Delete, Column	Deletes one or more columns
Range, Erase	to clear one or more cells and preserve the columns and rows
Worksheet, Erase	Clears the whole spreadsheet

- In the newly created D5 enter 'Minimum'. Then enter a set of numbers that will represent a minimum level of stock to be held before the company should order new stocks. Try the following numbers:

		Minimum
LM 233	Lawn Mower Delux	10
LM 236	Lawn Mower Standard	9
LM 240	Strimmer Super	9
LM 244	Hand Mower set	5
HC 101	Hedge Cutter	10
GH 21	Garden Hose 30m	15
GH 23	Garden Hose 50m	10
TL 100	Digging Tool	15
TL 105	Digging Spade	15
TL 110	Lawn Shears	15
TL 115	Border Fork	15
TL 120	Hand Shears	10
TL 125	Pruning Knife	10
WB 100	Wheelbarrow 3	

It should be easy to see that some, not all, stock items will not have the required minimum stock level. You need to include a column to show this.

Some of your spreadsheet will now be off the screen. This can cause a problem in that when you move too far to the right you will not be able to see what stock items you are dealing with. For now, put up with the problem, but you will see how to resolve the issue later.

- Set up a new column heading title at G3 called 'Shortfall' and widen column F as needed.

At cell G5 we would like to insert that if the actual stock amount (C5) is less than Minimum stock level (D5) then insert the Shortfall amount.

5.8 The IF function

Lotus provides an IF function which allows the value put into one cell to be made dependent on the content of another cell. The structure takes the following form:

@IF(X5>9,vtrue,vfalse) If the condition is true assign the value of vtrue, otherwise, that of vfalse. Vtrue and vfalse may be cell (or modified cell) values or numbers

- Go to G5 and enter '@IF(C5<D5,D5-C5,0)'.

You have stated that If C5<D5 (C5 is less than D5) then enter D5-C5, otherwise enter 0.

At cell G5 you want to insert that if the actual stock amount (C5) is less than Minimum stock level (D5) then insert the value 0 in this cell (G5).

- Use the Copy facility to replicate this formula from cell G5..G5 to the range G6..G18.

Setting up a window

In this activity you will produce a column that shows the percentage above the minimum stock level that current stock is at. Before starting, you want to find a way around the problem of not being able to see what stock you are referring to when you are at the right most side of the spreadsheet.

Lotus has a command that uses a window effect. Rather than try and explain it in too much detail, we encourage you to experiment with it.

- Move to any cell in column C.

- Select the command sequence Worksheet, Window.

You have, at present, the choice of creating a vertical or horizontal window. For this example use the vertical one.

- Select Vertical.

You will now see two spreadsheets appear. In fact it is the same spreadsheet appearing twice.

- Use F6 to make the cursor jump to the other window.

The use of F6 is solely for the purpose of moving between windows.

If you experiment with the cursor you will see that you can move around the spreadsheet in the current window position without altering the positioning in the other window. The only exception to this would be if you were to move a long way down the spreadsheet. Then the windows would move together. When spreadsheets become very large (as they often do), this facility can be useful.

If you want to keep your headings permanently in view, then you should set a horizontal window. Again F6 allows you to hop between windows.

Now back to determining the percentage stock above minimum.

- Go to H3 and enter the heading 'Surplus'. Again, you will need to adjust the width of column G.

The formula will be:

(Actual - Minimum) Divided by Minimum

At this stage you do not need to convert to a percentage by dividing by 100; let Lotus do that for you.

- Go to cell H5 and enter the formula '(C5-D5)/D5'.

This will leave you with a ratio rather than a percentage. The next stage is simply to format the range to a percentage.

- Use the command sequence /Range, Format, Percent to call the percentage format facility. Set the number of decimal places to 0 and then specify the range 'H5..H18'.

- Finally Copy the formula in the range H5..H5 to H6..H18.

At this stage it is worth questioning whether you want the negative values. If you do not, then how about using the IF statement in the following way in cell H5 and copying it through the required range?

@IF((C5-D5)/D5 > 0, (C5-D5)/D5, 0)

You will need to think about this one!!

- Now format the range H5.H18 to Percentages with zero decimal places.

5.9 Naming ranges

This activity will show you how to name a range of cells. Up to now you have learnt what a range of cells is. You will now learn about giving it a name. The purpose of this is that it is very much easier to remember the name of a range of cells rather than the co-ordinates of a range of cells. Using the example in this chapter, the column headed 'Stock value' should have the name 'values'.

- Move the cursor to cell F5. This is the starting point of the range.

- To achieve this call up Range from the Lotus menu and select Name from this sub-menu.

You should now see the see the text shown in screen dump 5.5.

On the top line you will see what is in the cell. In the example the cell is fixed to 2 decimal places (,2), is set at width 13 [W13] and is a formula +C6*E5.

- You want to create a range name, so press ENTER.

```
A: G5 (,Z) [W14] +C5×E5                                    MENU
Create  Delete  Labels  Reset  Table
Create or modify a range name
              B                F           G         H        I
```

Screen Dump 5.5

- You will now be asked for the range name. Enter the range name 'values'.

- Now specify the range as being 'G5..G18'.

Nothing will happen. In order to put this to some use, you will use the range name to calculate the total of all the values at the foot of the column.

- Go to cell G20 and enter the function '@sum(values)'.

This will have exactly the same effect as @SUM(F5..F18) which is the method you will be more familiar with from experience in earlier chapters.

More on the Name command

Going back to the Range, Name menu, there were four other options available which should now be explained. Look at screen dump 5.6.

```
A: G5 (,Z) [W14] +C5×E5                                    MENU
Create  Delete  Labels  Reset  Table
Create or modify a range name
              B                F           G         H        I
```

Screen Dump 5.6

Labels   This allows you to attach a label (name) to a whole series of range names. This will be more effectively used if you are using an exceptionally large spreadsheet that has a large number of range names created.

Delete   This allows you to delete a previously named range.

Reset   This deletes all previously named ranges from the spreadsheet.

Table   This sets up a table on the spreadsheet that lists all the named ranges and their cell locations. When you get to a situation where you have defined a large number of range names, this facility is useful to jog your memory about where things are. The table can be positioned where you want on the screen.

Please note that in both the cases of Delete and Reset, no data is erased from the spreadsheet, just the names of ranges.

Copying named ranges

Apart from using names to assist in the building of formulae, you can also use them to copy whole chunks of cells from part of the spreadsheet to another without specifying cell ranges. In fact wherever a situation arises where a cell range is asked for in the form XNN..XNN, it can be substituted for the range name. You can also use them in the following way:

● Press F5 and state that you want to go to 'values'.

This will take you to the first cell of the range in the top right position. Again, this makes it easier to decide where on the spreadsheet you wish to go.

As a way of emphasising the point:

● Go to H5 and create a range called 'surplus' comprising the range H5..H18.

● Now go to H20 and place the average surplus in this cell using the function '@AVG(surplus)'.

● Format this cell as a percentage to zero decimal places .

5.10 Chapter summary

It is worth noting that spreadsheets are often set up by people who have gained expertise in this area but are operated by others who simply want to look at the data and carry out simple operations. Good presentation is very important if someone without great skills in spreadsheet handling needs to extract information from them. In addition, you may find yourself returning to spreadsheets you have designed after a long absence. The situation can easily arise where you cannot find your way around your own spreadsheet if it is badly presented and muddled. Therefore it is important to consider presentation carefully.

In this chapter you have:

- Widened cells to allow text or numbers to fit
- Defined a range of cells and anchored at a cell when defining ranges
- Formatted a range of cells to a specified output requirement
- Copied formula ranges
- Presented text with differing justifications and centring
- Inserted and deleted columns or rows and erased ranges
- Setting up a window and moving between windows
- Used the IF function
- Named ranges and manipulated named ranges

6 DATES AND FORMULA

6.1 Aims of this chapter

This chapter concentrates on handling the Lotus date function by taking you through two worked examples. Additionally, it examines in closer detail how formula ranges can be copied from one part of a spreadsheet to another and still preserve the ability to execute calculations.

6.2 A worked example – Buying and Selling shares

This worked example is designed to show you more about writing formulae, manipulating dates, moving ranges and inserting rows and columns.

Screen dump 6.1 is what you are aiming for (note the three parts). You will set it up in a slightly different way across the screen so that you can move things around for practice.

6.3 Getting started

- Start with a blank spreadsheet and enter a company title – Handies Savings Trust will do but use any company name if you wish.

- Next enter identification labels. Use pointer keys to speed things up.

In cell	enter
A3	Purchase
A5	date
B5	shares
C5	price
D5	comm (3%)
E5	cost

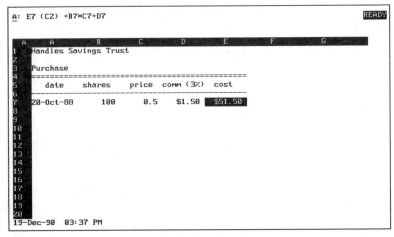

Screen Dump 6.1

- Centre the range of column labels A5 to E5 by moving to A5 and selecting the command sequence Range, Label, Centre. Highlight the range and the Press ENTER.

- Next create the double line that separates the column labels from the section heading. Move to A4 and enter '\=' (the reverse slash, \, is the repeat key). Then use the Copy command to copy this to B4..E4. Use the same procedure to copy the single line which separates the column labels from the numbers (see screen dump 6.1 again).

6.4 Entering dates

You will begin by entering the purchase date, October 20 1984. Usually, the date would be a label but here you want to perform some calculations with it such as determining how many days between purchase and sale. Can you think of other uses? To do this you use the @DATE function.

- Move to cell A7 and enter '@DATE(88,10,20)' i.e. Year, Month, Day.

The number 32436 should appear. If you have not already worked it out, this represents the number of days between January 1 1900 and October 10 1988. (Obvious really!) @DATE can convert dates between years 1900 and 2099. You will need to use the Date formatting facility in order to display the date in a way that can be understood.

- Select the command sequence Range, Format, Date and use the pointer keys to read the descriptions available. Accept the first option as shown in screen dump 6.2 which is DD-MMM-YY (Day-Month-Year) and at the prompt highlight the range for which you want the dates in this form; 'A7..A9' will do for now. The row of asterisks that appears in A7 means the column is not wide enough to accept the format. Widen the column (you should know how by now) until the date 20-Oct-90 appears.

- Move to B7 and enter '100', the number of shares purchased.

- Enter the share price of 0.5 (50 pence) in C7.

- In D7 enter the formula '+B7*C7*3%'.

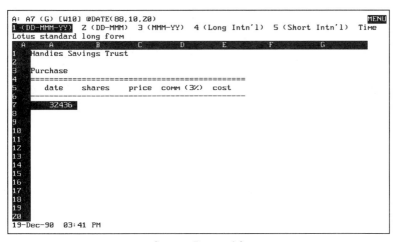

Screen Dump 6.2

Cell D7 should now show 1.50. If the figure is 1.49999.., then do not despair as it will soon be put right. You will need to change this format so that the amount is expressed as currency.

- Select the command sequence Range, Format, Currency and press ENTER to set the number of decimal places to 2. From here, format the range D7..E9 to indicate the figures are to be displayed as currency.

- Move to E7 and enter the formula '+B7*C7+D7'. What does this represent?

If you set the currency range correctly, it should include the cell E7 as currency and to 2 decimal places.

Check your work with screen dump 6.1. If you are satisfied, save it as HST1.

6.5 Copying a range

Examine the spreadsheet in screen dump 6.3 to see what you are aiming for next:

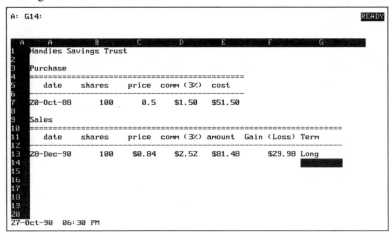

Screen Dump 6.3

- If you do not have the spreadsheet HST1 on screen, then load it now by entering the command sequence File, Retrieve and highlight the file name 'HST1' and press ENTER.

- Copy the column labels and lines (A4..E6) to F4.

6.6 Building up the spreadsheet _____

- Add the label 'Sale:' in F3 and change the label in J5 from 'cost' to 'amount'.

Now enter the sales data for HST.

- In F7 enter in @DATE format the date 'December 28th 1990'.

The number 33235 (the number of days between January 1 1900 and December 28 1990) should appear. To display numbers as dates in column F you will need to format cells F7..F9.

- Try formatting the dates now as suggested earlier.

28-Dec-86 should eventually appear in F7. the asterisks indicate that you need to widen a column to display data.

- Type 100 into G7, the number of shares, and the price per share in H7 (0.84).

- The broker's commission on the share sale is the same formula as used in D7. Try and copy this formula rather than simply typing it into the cell.

- Think up a formula in J7 to calculate the amount received from the share sale. If you do not end up with 81.48 in the cell then read the next instruction.

- The formula is '+G7*H7-I7' and is the selling price multiplied by the number of shares less the commission.

- Change the display format of the commission and cost figures to currency.

Note that the active area of your spreadsheet now goes further to the right than your screen allows you to see and you will have to move around the spreadsheet to see your work. The section on 'Sales' will be moved below the Purchases section later on.

This is now a useful time to practise skipping around.

- Get to cell A4, press the End key and then press the right arrow key once. This moves the pointer to J4, the furthest cell to the right with any data in it.

- Move to A1 by pressing the Home key and try pressing End followed by the down arrow key. This will take you down to the lowest row with data.

6.7 Moving a range

However much planning is done there is often a need to re-design a worksheet. There are many ways of shunting things around. For now concentrate on the Move command to bring the sales section below the purchases section so that you can see everything on the display screen. You can also print it as one single spreadsheet.

A range can be named then moved, but the initial approach will be to highlight what you want moved.

- Go to F3 and select the command Move. Highlight the range F3..J7 and press ENTER. You want to move the highlighted area to A9, so move the cursor to cell A9 and press ENTER.

Notice how you only needed to tell 123 where to start the TO range. Before commencing with the final section, save your spreadsheet as HST2.

You will now set up a section which will calculate the profit or loss from each completed transaction and determine whether the gain is 'long' or 'short' term. The criteria for determining whether a gain is long or short, is whether or not 365 days (one year) has lapsed between the purchase of shares and the selling of them. Examine screen dump 6.4 to see what you are aiming at.

- Enter the following into the cells:

```
A: C18:                                                    READY

  A      A          B        C        D        E        F        G
1  Handies Savings Trust
2
3  Purchase
4  ==================================================
5    date      shares    price   comm (3%)  cost
6  --------------------------------------------------
7  20-Oct-88    100      0.5     $1.50    $51.50
8  17-Feb-89    500      1.5     $22.50   $772.50
9  10-Aug-90    200      1       $6.00    $206.00
10
11 Sales
12 ===========================================================
13   date      shares    price   comm (3%)  amount  Gain (Loss) Term
14 ---------------------------------------------------------------
15 28-Dec-90    100     $0.84    $2.52    $81.48      $29.98 Long
16 28-Dec-90    250     $1.55    $11.63   $375.88   ($396.63)Long
17 28-Dec-90    200     $1.12    $6.72    $217.28     $11.28 Short
18
19
20
27-Oct-90   06:35 PM
```

Screen Dump 6.4

F11	Gain (Loss)
G11	Term

- Extend the double and single lines in rows 10 and 12 into columns F and G. Use the Copy command to do this.

Column F will be used to display gains or losses in amounts up to five figures.

- Set column F to Currency format and widen the column if necessary.

- In F13 type '+E13-E7'. This will be Sale price minus Purchase price.

6.8 Some decision making _____

The next job is to manipulate the date facilities.

- In G13 type '@IF(A13-A7>365,"Long","Short")'.

This means that if the difference between the dates in cells A13 and A7 is greater the 365 (one year) then print 'Long'. Otherwise print 'short'. Both 'Long' and 'Short' have been placed between parenthesis to indicate that they are labels and that they are to be right justified in the cell.

● Save your worksheet as HST3.

Examine screen dump 6.5 to see what the next objective is.

```
A:B19:                                                              READY

    A        A         B        C         D          E        F          G
  1    Caravan Sales for 1990      Mark up (%)     5.55
  2
  3    Month     No.Sold  Cost      Total          Selling  Profit
  4
  5       Jan-90       5    2,000       10,000       2,111     555
  6       Feb-90       4    2,000        8,000       2,111     444
  7       Mar-90       6    2,000       12,000       2,111     666
  8       Apr-90       8    2,300       18,400       2,428   1,021
  9       May-90      12    2,300       27,600       2,428   1,532
 10       Jun-90      17    2,300       39,100       2,428   2,170
 11       Jul-90      14    2,200       30,800       2,322   1,709
 12       Aug-90      10    2,100       21,000       2,217   1,166
 13       Sep-90       8    2,100       16,800       2,217     932
 14       Oct-90       7    2,100       14,700       2,217     816
 15       Nov-90       7    2,100       14,700       2,217     816
 16       Dec-90       5    2,100       10,500       2,217     583
 17
 18    TOTALS        103                                     12,410
 19
 20
27-Oct-90   06:45 PM
```

Screen Dump 6.5

Blank rows or columns can be created to tidy up presentation or to fit extra data. You will now enter data for two more share purchases and sales.

● Move to A8 and select the command sequence Worksheet, Insert, Row) and then highlight A8..A9 and ENTER.

This will create two new rows. Using the command sequence /Worksheet, Delete will delete rows or columns from the worksheet.

● Make up your own data or use that shown in screen dump 6.4.

Cells used should be A8, B8, C8 and A16, B16, C16. You will have to format the data cells and remember that it is quicker and easier to copy formula rather than keep typing them in. Also, you can copy more than one formula at a time; for example

Range to copy FROM: D7..G7.

Range to copy TO: D15..G15.

● Now save your worksheet as HST, print it out and delete worksheets HST1 and HST2.

The figure inside the brackets indicates that it is negative and in our example this means a loss.

At this stage you should experiment with the figures to see how the numbers change when for example you change the number of shares and how the Term type changes when you alter the dates.

In this example, you may have observed that whenever you copy or moved ranges of formulae, the calculations always remain correct. The next short example will show you that this is not always so and you will need to define some formulae in a slightly different way.

6.9 Relative versus Absolute formula

This next example uses a list of dates and numbers of caravans sold by a particular dealer in the year 1990. Examine screen dump 6.6 before starting to see exactly what you are trying to achieve.

```
A:  E5:  (,0)  +C5*$E$1/100+C5                                          READY

         A          B        C          D           E        F         G
1   Caravan Sales for 1990        Mark up (%)      5.55
2
3   Month      No.Sold   Cost      Total      Selling  Profit
4
5       Jan-90      5      2,000       10,000    2,111      555
6       Feb-90      4      2,000        8,000    2,111      444
7       Mar-90      6      2,000       12,000    2,111      666
8       Apr-90      8      2,300       18,400    2,428    1,021
9       May-90     12      2,300       27,600    2,428    1,532
10      Jun-90     17      2,300       39,100    2,428    2,170
11      Jul-90     14      2,200       30,800    2,322    1,709
12      Aug-90     10      2,100       21,000    2,217    1,166
13      Sep-90      8      2,100       16,800    2,217      932
14      Oct-90      7      2,100       14,700    2,217      816
15      Nov-90      7      2,100       14,700    2,217      816
16      Dec-90      5      2,100       10,500    2,217      583
17
18  TOTALS        103                                    12,410
19
20
04-Jan-91   11:41 AM
```

Screen Dump 6.6

The mark up of 5.5% will be used to determine the selling price of the caravans. Each month a number of caravans are sold such as 10 in August. They cost £2,200 each which is a total cost of 22,000. The 5.5% mark up gives a selling price 2,322 per caravan. The profit is worked out as the difference between Selling and Cost price multiplied by the Number Sold.

Setting up the spreadsheet

- Put your heading 'Caravan Sales for 1990' in A1 and 'Mark up (%)' in cell D1.

- The column headings with cell locations are:

Month	A3	
No. sold	B3	
Cost	C3	
Total	D3	(you will need to widen column D)
Selling	E3	
Profit	F3	

- Enter all the numbers sold in column B for the range B5..B16 and the costs in column C for the range C5..C16. Also enter the text 'TOTALS' in cell A18.

- In cell E1 enter the number 5.5. This will be the percentage that is added to the Cost price to arrive at the selling price.

Some further use of @DATE

Now you can concentrate on entering formulae into cells in an efficient way.

Start by entering the months.

- Go to cell A5 and, using the @DATE function, enter the date for 1st January 1990. The number 32874 should appear, the number of days between January 1 1900 and January 1 1990. Format this cell and the range to A16 to show the date format as MMM-YY.

- Now move down to cell A6 and enter the formula '+A5+31'.

The purpose of this is to add 31 days to the previous month's figure in order to move from January to February.

- Now use the copy facility to Copy the formula FROM A6..A6 TO A7..A16.

Each consecutive month should appear from January to December. This would not work if you ran into many years of rows because most months have less than 31 days in them. However, the principle is that in each cell containing the formula, it is derived by being 31 higher than the cell above.

- At this stage, browse through the cells and examine each formula in the range A5..A16 and be clear in your own mind about what has happened.

The effects of having relative cell formulae _____

This principle of formulae always taking a relative set of values is an important one. Look again to see how the concept works.

- Go to D5 where you will calculate the total cost of the caravans to the trader. The formula will be '+C5*B5'.

- Now copy the formula FROM D5..D5 TO D6..D16.

Again observe what has happened in the cells in this range. Each formula is a multiple of the cell two positions to the left and one cell to the left.

Now you will see where this principle is not what is wanted in determining the selling price. The formula you want in E5 is one that multiples the cost price (C5) by the percentage mark up (E1) divided by 100 and then added to the original cost (C5).

- Go to E5 and enter the formula '+(C5*E1/100)+C5'.

- Now try and copy the formula from E5..E5 to E6..E16.

Something has gone wrong!

Observe the formula in the cells and you will see that the percentage to work with (5.5%) is always assumed to be four cells directly above.

In fact, although this relative position has worked in your favour up until now, you want to fix the cell E1 in the formula. This is called defining an **absolute** cell value and is done by placing a $ (dollar) sign in front of the cell location; in other words instead of placing E1 in the formula you should have place '$E$1' in the formula.

- Return to cell E5 and enter the formula '+(C5*$E$1/100)+C5'.

- Now copy the formula FROM E5..E5 TO E6..E16

You now have the desired result.

- To complete the spreadsheet, type in the remaining formula in cell F5, '(E5-C5)*B5', and copy this to the range F6..F16.

- At the foot of column B in cell B18 is the function '@SUM(B5..B16)'. Having placed this function into cell B18 it can be copied to cell D18 (range D18..D18). After this you can again copy the formulae to cell F18.

Copying cells from one cell to another can still be quicker and less prone to error than placing formulae into cells individually.

- In order to tidy up your spreadsheet format all the money values should be to the nearest whole number and using commas to separate the thousands.

Change the number in E1 to see the instant effect.

- Save your spreadsheet for possible future reference and practice.

6.10 Summary _____

As a brief concluding challenge to this chapter, try this problem:

Allow cell F18 (Total Profit) to be entered by the user. from this, the spreadsheet should determine the percentage mark up that is needed to get to this profit and will then state the price that should be charged for the caravans each month.

In this chapter you have:

- Manipulated text around the spreadsheet

- Entered dates using the @DATE function
- Formatted dates and currencies
- Met new techniques of moving around the spreadsheet
- Copied relative formulae
- Set absolute cell locations in formulae and copied such formulae
- Used the @IF function to make decisions
- Moved ranges

7 DATABASES

7.1 Aims of this chapter _____

This chapter examines the way Lotus 123 allows you to set up data tables and sort them into an order. In doing so, it also examines a method whereby a table can be rearranged by a single operation from the user rather than a whole series of command entries through Lotus menus.

In many cases it is useful to extract certain information from a data table such as a list of all unsold houses in a list of house details held by an estate agent. This example is developed in the latter part of this chapter.

7.2 Setting out a database table _____

Screen dump 7.1 will show you what you are trying to achieve in this chapter.

```
A:AZ0: [W22] 'N - By Surname   D - By Date of Birth   S - By Salary            READY

            A              B         C         D         E         F
1    St Eastleigh Borough Council
2
3    Employees in Works Department
4
5    Surname of Employee    Initials Date of Birth      Salary
6    ========================================================================
7    Davidson               R        25-Dec-60          12090
8    Evans                  W        13-May-70          10900
9    Hammonds               E        30-Mar-71           9900
10   Harriets               M N      12-Dec-51          15300
11   Montgomery             F        08-Aug-46           9637
12   Redbrook               A D      20-Oct-67           9000
13   Shrewsbury             D R      19-Oct-63          14000
14   Style                  A J      14-Nov-55          12090
15   Villiers               W        03-Sep-59          11500
16   Westcourt              K        22-Oct-68          21002
17   ========================================================================
18   TO SORT TABLE PRESSING Alt KEY AND SINGLE CHARACTER KEY TOGETHER
19
20   N - By Surname    D - By Date of Birth   S - By Salary
24-Oct-90   10:21 AM
```

Screen Dump 7.1

The instructions on the screen informs the operator that by pressing Alt and D simultaneously they can rearrange the data so that each line appears in Date of Birth order rather than, as appears above, in Surname order. In other words, in one key stroke you get from screen dump 7.1 to screen dump 7.2 with the titles and footers still on screen.

When lists are exceptionally long, this facility is extremely useful. Also, if a single employee has to be added to the list, then you need only create a new line on the spreadsheet, insert the details and use the Alt key command to rearrange the list back into sorted order.

Before starting it is worth making yourself familiar with some of the jargon that this chapter will introduce you to.

A database is a collection of records. In the example the database is a collection of employee records stating name, date of birth and salary. In fact for each employee there is a single **record** that is a collection of four **fields**; one field each for Surname, Initial, Date of Birth and Salary.

```
A:A20: [W22] 'N - By Surname  D - By Date of Birth  S - By Salary        READY

                A              B          C           D       E        F
1   St Eastleigh Borough Council
2
3   Employees in Works Department
4
5   Surname of Employee    Initials Date of Birth      Salary
6   ===================================================================
7   Montgomery             F        08-Aug-46            9637
8   Harriets               M N      12-Dec-51           15300
9   Style                  A J      14-Nov-55           12090
10  Villiers               W        03-Sep-59           11500
11  Davidson               R        25-Dec-60           12090
12  Shrewsbury             D R      19-Oct-63           14000
13  Redbrook               A D      20-Oct-67            9000
14  Westcourt              K        22-Oct-68           21002
15  Evans                  W        13-May-70           10900
16  Hammonds               E        30-Mar-71            9900
17  ===================================================================
18  TO SORT TABLE PRESSING Alt KEY AND SINGLE CHARACTER KEY TOGETHER
19
20  N - By Surname   D - By Date of Birth  S - By Salary
24-Oct-90  10:25 AM
```

Screen Dump 7.2

Later in this chapter, in an attempt to impress on you the terms, a different database is set up which will have a different number of records and each record will have a different number of fields.

7.3 Entering record details _____

- Load 123 and start by entering the required header labels that are to appear on the screen.

Cell	Label
A1	St Eastleigh Borough Council
A3	Employees in Works Department
A5	Surname of Employee
B5	Initials
C5	Date of Birth
E5	Salary

- Enter into cell A6 '\=' and copy this across the screen by the sequence of command /C and copying FROM A6..A6 TO B6..E6.

- In order to see what is in the cells, you will have to widen the columns for column A and column C. A width of 22 for A and 11 for C will be sufficient. You should know how to do this by now.

Next will appear the details of each individual employee. Each line, or row, on the spreadsheet represents a record of an employee with the cell locations holding the fields Surname, Initials, Date of Birth and Salary.

- Enter the record details, remembering that dates will have to be entered in function form such as @DATE(60,12,25). From this you will have to format the date using the command sequence Range, Format, Date.

At this point, it may be worth your while entering the records in a different and unsorted order.

- Enter '\=' into cell A17 and copy this across the screen in the same manner as you did for Row 6.

● Now complete the labels for screen display:

Into Cell A18 enter the label: 'TO SORT TABLE PRESSING Alt KEY AND SINGLE CHARACTER KEY TOGETHER'

and into cell A20 enter the label:

'N - By Surname D - By Date of birth S - By Salary'

In your database you must ensure that:

1 The column heading represents the Field name.

2 That each field name is unique, i.e. does not appear twice.

3 That each record is kept on one row.

7.4 Sorting the records

The next task is to rearrange the records into surname order.

● From the menu, call the data facilities using the command /Data. From the options available, you want to sort the records into order, so select Sort.

At this point you need to define where on the spreadsheet the data range is. Although you know where the data range is, the computer will not be able to distinguish between this and the headings.

● Select Data-Range and enter the required range where the data records are stored; 'A7..E16' and then press ENTER.

Screen dump 7.3 shows how, using the principle of pointing, anchoring and highlighting, the Data-Range to be sorted is selected.

Having defined where the data range is, the next stage is to indicate by what field you want to sort the records, i.e. the primary-key field.

● Select Primary-key to indicate you want to define the primary-key field to sort by. Enter a range 'A7..A16' to mark where this field is, that is the surname field that you want to sort by. When you have selected this press ENTER. You will now be asked in what order

```
A:E16: Z100Z                                                    POINT
Enter Data-Range: A7..E16

         A              B         C          D        E       F
1   St Eastleigh Borough Council
2
3   Employees in Works Department
4
5   Surname of Employee   Initials Date of Birth      Salary
6   ========================================================
7   Davidson              R        25-Dec-60           12090
8   Evans                 W        13-May-70           10900
9   Hammonds              E        30-Mar-71            9900
10  Harriets              M N      12-Dec-51           15300
11  Montgomery            F        08-Aug-46            9637
12  Redbrook              A D      20-Oct-67            9800
13  Shrewsbury            D R      19-Oct-63           14000
14  Style                 A J      14-Nov-55           12090
15  Villiers              W        03-Sep-59           11500
16  Westcourt             K        22-Oct-68           Z100Z
17  ========================================================
18  TO SORT TABLE PRESSING Alt KEY AND SINGLE CHARACTER KEY TOGETHER
19
20  N - By Surname   D - By Date of Birth  S - By Salary
24-Oct-90  10:26 AM
```

Screen Dump 7.3

you want the records to appear, ascending or descending; enter Ascending.

In the event that two surnames are the same, you want to decide on what basis to sort the common records by. This is when you define the Secondary-key field.

● Select Secondary-key to indicate you want to define the secondary key field to sort by. Enter a range 'B7..B16' to mark where this field is, that is the Initials field that you want to sort by in the event of two or more surnames being the same. When you have selected this press ENTER. You will now be asked in what order you want the records to appear, ascending or descending; enter Ascending.

● Now enter Go and you will see the effect.

Experiment with this by changing the surname orders and repeating the process. If you were to list the order in which the commands were entered, using a '~' sign (tilde) to indicate when the ENTER key has to be pressed, you get the following sequence:

/DSDA7..E16~PA7..A16~A~SB7..B16~A~G

Try it out now.

If you are unsure where your '~' symbol is on your keyboard, then find out now – you will need it later.

7.5 Sorting in different orders

The next step is to attempt to do much the same thing but to organise the records in a different order. In the next example you will attempt to arrange the records in Date of Birth order.

● Attempt the following sequence of commands in order to sort the records by Date of Birth order:

/DSDA7..E16~PC7..C16~A~SA7..A16~A~G

By now you should have got the idea that it is possible, given the correct sequence of commands, that fairly sophisticated operations on a spreadsheet can be achieved.

● Try this sequence:

/DSDA7..E16~PE7..E16~D~SA7..A16~A~G

The effect of this is to sort the record into descending salary order; that is, the lowest value is at the top of the list, and the highest at the bottom.

Try and understand what is going on before proceeding to the next section. As a way of understanding, you should keep experimenting with changing the way the order record appears.

7.6 Using macros

The next stage is to build a facility into the spreadsheet whereby an operator does not have to enter such a sophisticated sequence of commands in order to alter the logical sequence of records on the screen as and when needed. In other words, you want to replace a sequence of commands with just one key stroke.

The concept you need is a **macro**, a facility of storing all these commands somewhere on a spreadsheet that can be activated by an operator with only one command.

The stages are to:

1   Store the macro somewhere on the spreadsheet, preferably out of sight.

2   Store in the cell the label that represents the sequence of events. This forms the macro.

3   Name the macro. When naming the macro, it will be prefixed with '\' followed by one single character.

You can now create the first of these macros to sort the database records by Name order in the stages indicated.

● Use key F5 and go to cell A90.

● Now place the macro as a label in the cell. You must start the entry with ' (an apostrophe). The cell should have the label '/DSDA7..E16~PA7..A16~A~SB7..B16~A~G'.

● Name the cell as P using the command sequence Range, Name, Create and Name the range A90..A90 as '\P'. Be careful about using the correct slash (\) key.

The macro is now ready. When you press the Alt and P simultaneously the macro name \P will be executed; that is, Name is sorted into Surname order.

Next you need a macro to sort the database into Date of Birth order.

● Use F5 and go to cell A95.

● Place the macro as a label in the cell as

    /DSDA7..E16~PC7..C16~A~SA7..A16~A~G

● Now name the cell as 'D' using the command sequence Range, Name, Create and Name the range A95..A95 as '\D'.

And finally, you want a macro to sort names by Salary order.

● Use key F5 and go to cell A100.

● Place the macro as a label in the cell as

/DSDA7..E16~PE7..E16~D~SA7..A16~A~G

● Name the cell as 'S' using the command sequence Range, Name, Create and Name the range A100..A100 as '\S'.

Now save your work under the name 'dbase1' and experiment with the three macros you have set up.

By now, you should have gained a reasonable understanding of what a macro is and how to set one up and use it. The next section of this chapter will give some more details about the database facilities contained within Lotus 123, and the next chapter covers in greater detail the use of macros.

7.7 Using Data Query on a database

In this part of the chapter, you will use the Data Query part of the program as a way of extracting certain attributes about a data table. Examine screen dump 7.4.

The aim is quite simple: to extract from the table a list of all those houses that have not been sold.

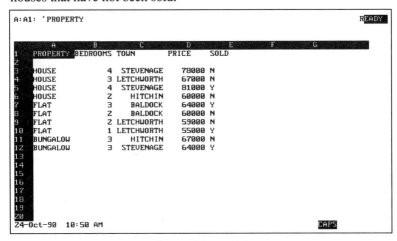

Screen Dump 7.4

Start by acquainting yourself with some more jargon. What you actually want to do is set up a **query table** to which we will copy required data. For Release 3 users it would make a lot of sense to copy required data into another spreadsheet. However, in this chapter you will use another part of the spreadsheet as a query table. The **criteria** section will represent the table from which you want to select the data.

- Begin by entering these details, as shown, into their respective cells on the spreadsheet. You will need to widen some columns.

In the screen dump the command sequence Range, Label has been used to Right Justify the Town names in column 'C'. If you want to achieve this then:

- Use Range, Label and Right from the command sequence to select right justify followed by entering the range C3..C12.

- Now use the menu system to get to Data Query. From here use the Input option and define the Input-Range as A1..E12.

At this stage you will have defined your Database range as being the block bounded by the area from cell A1 to E12. Each row (house detail) represents a single record in the database range, while each cell in a row represents a field. In the example you have ten records from row 3 to 12 and each record has five fields from column A to F. This is a simple principle well worth getting used to. At the top of each column is the field name, which will have an important part to play in the demonstration.

Screen dump 7.5 shows how the Input-Range is highlighted. It is also important to note that the Input-Range must include the field names at the top of the column. This is different to the Data-Range used earlier to sort data as it excluded the field names.

7.8 Defining a Criteria-Range _____

The next stage is to enter details about a Criteria-Range. This is what the program needs to determine what you selected from the database. In the example you will work on the basis of selecting details of all unsold houses.

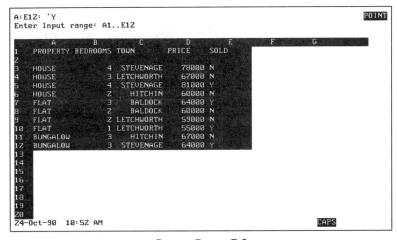

```
A:E1Z: 'Y                                                      POINT
Enter Input range: A1..E1Z

        A       B       C        D       E     F       G
1   PROPERTY BEDROOMS TOWN     PRICE    SOLD
2
3   HOUSE        4   STEVENAGE  78000 N
4   HOUSE        3   LETCHWORTH 67000 N
5   HOUSE        4   STEVENAGE  81000 Y
6   HOUSE        2   HITCHIN    60000 N
7   FLAT         3   BALDOCK    64000 Y
8   FLAT         2   BALDOCK    60000 N
9   FLAT         2 LETCHWORTH   59000 N
10  FLAT         1 LETCHWORTH   55000 Y
11  BUNGALOW     3   HITCHIN    67000 N
12  BUNGALOW     3   STEVENAGE  64000 Y
13
14
15
16
17
18
19
20
24-Oct-90   10:52 AM                                         CAPS
```

Screen Dump 7.5

- Set up the Criteria-Range by first entering into the respective cells the following details.

	G
1	SOLD
2	N

You use this to tell you that what you are interested in (Criterion) is those records where the field name 'SOLD' has an 'N' entered. What you now want to do is to set up a Criteria-Range; in other words give the computer a reference point.

- From the Data Query menu select the Criteria option and define as the Input criterion the range 'G1..G2'.

It is important that the Criteria-Range includes the field name that appears at the top of the column where the data is held.

7.9 Defining an Output-Range

The next stage is to decide where to put records you select. This is called the Output-Range.

● Enter the following details in their respective cells:

Cell	Location Label
A15	PROPERTY
B15	BEDROOMS
C15	TOWN
D15	PRICE
E15	SOLD

● From the Data Query menu select the Output option and define the Output-Range as 'A15..E25'.

This range goes well below the field names that have been set up on row 15. The purpose of this is to make sure that there is ample space to place the fields of houses we want selected from the Criteria-Range. Placing the Output-Range underneath the Input-Range has the advantage of the column widths already being set up correctly, there is no imperative need for this.

You will also observe that the Output-Range needs the field names at the top. Each field name must match one in the Input-Range and does not necessarily need to be in the same order.

7.10 Extracting the required data

● From the Data Query menu select the Extract option.

As a result of this action you should have achieved the results shown in screen dump 7.6.

Now try the following:

● Redefine your criterion range as:

```
A15: 'PROPERTY                                                    MENU
Input  Criterion  Output  Find  Extract  Unique  Delete  Reset  Quit
Copy all records that match criteria to Output range
        A         B         C        D        E      F        G
1   PROPERTY BEDROOMS TOWN       PRICE    SOLD          SOLD
2                                                        N
3   HOUSE        4   STEVENAGE   78000 N
4   HOUSE        3   LETCHWORTH  67000 N
5   HOUSE        4   STEVENAGE   81000 Y
6   HOUSE        2    HITCHIN    60000 N
7   FLAT         3    BALDOCK    64000 Y
8   FLAT         2    BALDOCK    60000 N
9   FLAT         2  LETCHWORTH   59000 N
10  FLAT         1  LETCHWORTH   55000 Y
11  BUNGALOW     3    HITCHIN    67000 N
12  BUNGALOW     3   STEVENAGE   64000 Y
13
14
15  PROPERTY BEDROOMS TOWN       PRICE    SOLD
16  HOUSE        4   STEVENAGE   78000 N
17  HOUSE        3   LETCHWORTH  67000 N
18  HOUSE        2    HITCHIN    60000 N
19  FLAT         2    BALDOCK    60000 N
20  FLAT         2  LETCHWORTH   59000 N
24-Oct-90   10:57 AM                                        CAPS
```

Screen Dump 7.6

	G
1	PRICE
2	+D3<64000

- From the Data Query menu select the Extract option.

This has the effect of extracting all houses with a price of less than £64,000. When placing this formula into the cell you will see that a zero will be placed into the cell. This indicates that the condition is false; in other words, the zero (0) reveals that the cell value is NOT less than 64000. When you extract from this, the operation knows to perform this throughout the INPUT list. Redefine your Criteria-Range as:

	G	H
1	PROPERTY	BEDROOMS
2	HOUSE	+B3>2

115 ■

● From the Data Query menu select the Extract option

The effect should be to extract those properties which are houses with more than two bedrooms.

7.11 Finding and deleting selected Records _____

Now have a look at a facility that allows you to search and locate records based on a given criteria.

● Redefine your Criteria-Range as:

G

1	PRICE
2	+D3<64000

● Select FIND from the Data Query menu to locate the first record in your Input-Range that meets this criteria. In other words, the first property with a price greater than £60,000.

Before going any further, it would be wise to save your spreadsheet in case you ever want to refer back to it.

● Reset the Criteria section to:

G

1	SOLD
2	N

● Select Extract from the Data Query menu to place into the Output table a copy of those fields whose houses have not been sold.

Before deleting records, it is often a good idea to save the current version of the spreadsheet in case it is needed again.

● From the Data Query menu select Delete.

This will have the effect of deleting from the Input range all records that match the Criteria-Range. In other words, it will remove all records that have 'N' in the SOLD field. As a precaution, you will be asked whether you want to cancel the request or delete it. When you delete there is no going back.

● Enter Delete in response.

From screen dump 7.7 you will see that all the records with 'N' in the SOLD field appear in the output table while all the records without 'N' in the SOLD field appear in the input table.

```
A15: 'PROPERTY                                                          MENU
Input   Criterion   Output   Find   Extract   Unique   Delete   Reset   Quit
Delete all records that match criteria
         A        B         C          D        E        F        G
1   PROPERTY BEDROOMS TOWN       PRICE      SOLD           SOLD
2                                                          N
3   HOUSE          4   STEVENAGE   81000 Y
4   FLAT           3     BALDOCK   64000 Y
5   FLAT           1 LETCHWORTH    55000 Y
6   BUNGALOW       3   STEVENAGE   64000 Y
7
8
9
10
11
12
13
14
15  PROPERTY BEDROOMS TOWN       PRICE      SOLD
16  HOUSE          4   STEVENAGE   78000 N
17  HOUSE          3 LETCHWORTH    67000 N
18  HOUSE          2     HITCHIN   60000 N
19  FLAT           2     BALDOCK   60000 N
20  FLAT           2 LETCHWORTH    59000 N
24-Oct-90   11:00 AM                               CALC           CAPS
```

Screen Dump 7.7

7.12 Further work with database

In this third example you will attempt to set up a simple stock database and from it, sort the list of records in value order or stock reference order and print a list in stock number order.

To get yourself started examine screen dump 7.8 to see what kind of layout is required and the cell entries you want, observing the following points:

```
A:G4                                                              READY

         A          B          C          D          E          F          G
1  Stock Records      Sort keys: Alt-R by Reference     Alt-V by Value
2                            /dsda6..f16~pa6..a16~a~g      /dsda6..f16~pf6..f16~a~
3  Stock        Quantity Unit       Reorder    Reorder   Stock
4  Reference             Cost       Level      Quantity  Value
5
6  A100              12      1.89        10          8    22.68
7  C777              74      0.56        50         30    41.44
8  A224              15      2.80        12         10    42.00
9  D100              34      1.62        40         20    55.08
10 B109               8      9.00        10          5    72.00
11 A321              32      2.99        35         20    95.68
12 D220              32      3.33        30         15   106.56
13 A343              20     10.00        20         10   200.00
14 B652              32      7.01        30         20   224.32
15 B767              22     12.88        20         10   283.36
16 B200              16     55.00        10         10   880.00
17
18                                                       2023.12
19
20
24-Oct-90  06:52 PM
```

Screen Dump 7.8

- The field Stock Reference has label entries.

- The fields Quantity, Unit Cost, Reorder Level and Reorder Quantity are Numeric entries.

- Stock Value is a formula entry made up of the Quantity multiplied by the Unit Cost.

- Cell F18 is a @SUM function summing all Stock Values.

- The numbers in both column C and F are formatted to two decimal places using the command sequence Range, Format, Fixed.

- Cells C2 and F2 contain the sorting macros named 'R' and 'V' respectively.

7.13 Hiding data

An obvious problem with the spreadsheet as it stands is the display of the two macros. Before you simply placed the macro in a part of the spreadsheet that was out of the way. A better method may be to leave it where it is but hide it from the screen.

- From the main menu select the command sequence Range, Format and Hide.

- After selecting Hide, enter the range to be hidden 'C2..F2'.

The functioning of the macro or anything else in a cell is completely unaffected by hiding it.

7.14 A macro for printing

You shall try printing the worksheet database in stock number order. As you already have a macro for sorting the records into stock number order, you ought to take advantage of this first.

- Copy the cell range C2..C2 into G4..G4.

Although the cell contents of C2 were hidden, they still copied into a cell which leaves them visible. This represents the first macro. In cell G5 you will enter the print macro.

Your printing macro should only print the database details rather than the whole spreadsheet. A macro that will achieve this is:

\PPRA3..F18~AG

- Enter the macro into cell G5.

- Using the command sequence Range, Name give the cell range G4..G5 the name '\P'.

- Now activate the macro using Alt-P.

- To keep the spreadsheet tidy, hide the new macro.

We have now got a macro of two sequences of commands. Lotus will assume that when a named macro has a range like this, then it will carry on down a list of such sequences from the beginning of a range to the end.

7.15 Setting up an Output-Range on another sheet

This section is aimed at Lotus Release 3 Users and introduces multiple spreadsheets, which is covered in detail in chapter 10. In this instance you are going to set up an Output-Range on another spreadsheet, but still visible on the screen.

At the top left corner of your screen, the contents of the current cell have always been prefixed with 'A:' which indicates that you are working with 'A' sheet. We shall create another one as 'B' sheet.

● Select Worksheet from the command menu followed by Insert and the select Sheet.

This will leave you with the option of inserting another worksheet before or after the existing one on the screen.

● Enter After so that the current sheet appears at the front when seeing them all at one time.

The new worksheet now appears on the screen.

● Press the Alt key and the key F6 simultaneously to show both sheets, A and B.

When placing records into an Output-Range you will set the Output-Range within sheet B. This has the benefit of allowing any size of output to be sent to sheet B as there is nothing getting in the way. This advantage becomes more apparent as the size of the database becomes bigger.

One problem you will face is that the field names at the top of each column will not help you perform the task. What you need to achieve is unique field names in one cell.

● Replace the labels in row 4 as follows

B4	with	QTY	(currently blank)
D4	with	ROL	(currently 'Level')
E4	with	ROQ	(currently 'Value')

● Now use the command /Copy to copy FROM A:A4..F4 TO B:A1..F1.

You now have a set of common field names for both the INPUT and OUTPUT ranges. Again, it is important that each field name at the top of an Output-Range can be matched with one at the top of an Input-Range. Now you will define the Input-and Output-Ranges.

- From the Data, Query menu select the Input option and define the INPUT RANGE as 'A:A6..F16'.

- From the Data, Query menu select the Output option and define the OUTPUT RANGE as 'B:A1..F10'.

Be careful not to omit the A: or B: prefix that determines the sheets involved.

Now you need to set up a Criteria-Range in sheet A. You have to copy all records from the Input-Range to the Output-Range where the Quantity is below the reorder level. As the fields are labelled as QTY and ROL respectively you will need to enter the Criteria-Range as +QTYTo make life a little easier, enter a new column in G which states the difference between the Quantity and Reorder level.

- Enter into cell G4 of Sheet A the label 'DIFF'.

- Enter into cell G6 of Sheet A the formula +D6-B6.

- Copy the formula from A:G6..G6 to A:G7..G16.

Now you simply need to send records where the DIFF is negative, in other words, when you are below the Reorder level.

- Enter into the cell range at A:A18;

	G
1	SOLD
2	N

- Select Extract from the Data Query menu to place into the Output table a copy of those fields whose DIFF is less than zero.

Move your cell pointer into your 'B' sheet and enter columns next to your Output-Range for calculating the costs of reordering (Reorder quantity multiplied by Unit Cost).

7.16 Summary

In this chapter, you will have:

- Defined the term database, record and field

- Entered a structured database with records on rows and field titles at the top columns

- Practised further with Worksheet, Copy, Range and File commands

- Sorted records into logical sequences

- Set up, named and activated a macro

- Set up a query and extracted data from a defined Input-Range into an Output-Range using a given criterion

- Located a record from an Input-Range using given criteria

- Deleted records from an Input-Range using given criteria

- Hidden cells from the screen

- Written a macro made up of two different sequences of commands

- Set up a multiple spreadsheet and defined an Output-Range in another sheet

8 FURTHER ON GRAPHS

8.1 Aims of this chapter

This chapter aims to give you some more practice with graphs and to take your knowledge beyond that developed in chapter 4. Lotus offers a range of different style of graphs which the chapter investigates further.

Because so many other skills have been tackled since this chapter was covered, it is assumed that much of the work in setting up a spreadsheet can be done by you without too much guidance.

In exploring the capabilities of the graphics contained in Lotus, you will need to refer back to chapter 4 if you need help with printing your graphs. This chapter will not return to the processes of graph printing. Some references about more advanced printing will be covered in the next chapter.

8.2 More on bar charts

This section explores bar charts using a different example from that set out in chapter 4. Screen dump 8.1 shows a spreadsheet of an insurance company's premiums over a given year.

The location of the labels should be apparent. However, with respect to the numbers, you have to enter the data into the cells observing the following the following:

- The insurance groupings Motor, Property, Life, Marine and Other are right justified using the command sequence Range, Label Right.

- Numeric values in each premium collected for each City office are in the range B8..G8.

```
A:B8: (,0) 12000                                                    READY

       A          B        C       D      E       F        G        H
1  XANIPAN INSURANCE BROKERS
2
3  Premiums Collected  - 1990
4
5
6               Motor  Property  Life  Marine  Other   TOTALS Percentage
7
8  Bristol      12,000   6,000   5,000   3,500   1,300   27,800      16%
9  Cardiff       9,500   5,500   5,100   1,200   1,200   22,500      13%
10 Glasgow      10,000   4,800   4,300   2,300   1,700   23,100      13%
11 London       18,000  11,300  10,500   4,200   3,400   47,400      27%
12 Manchester   13,000   5,900   4,600   1,400   1,100   26,000      15%
13 Norwich      13,500   6,700   6,200     900   1,300   28,600      16%
14
15 TOTALS       76,000  40,200  35,700  13,500  10,000  175,400     100%
16
17 Percentage      43%     23%     20%      8%      6%     100%
18
19
20
25-Oct-90   09:51 AM
```

Screen Dump 8.1

- The totals are all derived using the @SUM function.

- All monetary values are formatted with a comma to zero decimal places.

- Column widths are adjusted to show up the City Office names and fit into column H in the spreadsheet.

- The percentages are derived using a formula. The formula in H8 is +G8/$G$15 and in cell B17 is +B15/$G$15.

The use of the dollar sign in the formula sets the cell G15 in the formula as an absolute cell rather than a relative one. This allows us to copy the cell formula from cell H8..H8 to H9..H13 and to copy the formula from cell B17..B17 to C17..G17.

- All the percentage figures are formatted as a percentage to zero decimal places using the command sequence Range, Format, Percent.

Now to working on the graph.

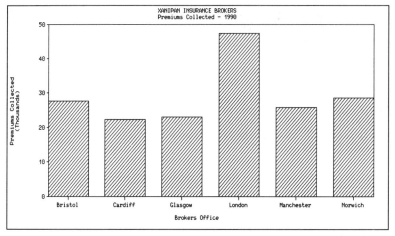

Graph 8.1

Graph 8.1 shows a graph that is no different in construction to the one set up in chapter 4. However, it will prove a useful starting point. As a general principle, use the following procedure for preparing a graph:

1 Prepare that initial data in the spreadsheet.

2 Determine the type of graph required.

3 Identify the X variable. In other words what you want to measure the numbers against. In graph 8.1 the premiums collected are shown against Brokers Office. Consequently, Brokers Office becomes the X variable.

4 Determine the Y variable(s). In graph 8.1 this is the TOTAL premiums collected by that particular office.

5 Give the graph a title to appear on the graph when it is printed.

6 If applicable, attach a description on the X-axis and Y-axis to describe what is being measured. In graph 8.1 it is clear that you are looking at the amount of premiums (Y-axis) being collected against each Broker Office (X-axis).

7 If applicable, enter legends on the graph. Later you will see that when you have a series of bars against each Broker Office, a legend will help us see what each bar represents.

8 Create a name for the graph. Release 2 users will need to save the graph with a file name for later printing.

9 If required, print the graph.

10 If required, change the numbers in the spreadsheet and repeat stages 8 and 9.

11 If required, reset the graph and go back to 2 in this list; otherwise save the spreadsheet and quit.

With all of these stages in mind, you can now reproduce the graph shown in graph 8.1.

● Select the command sequence /Graph, Type, Bar to choose a Bar chart.

The X variable will be the name of the brokers' offices which appear in the cell range A8..A13.

● Select X and enter the X Range A8..A13.

● Now select the A Range and enter the range that represents the totals for each of these offices in cells G8..G13

While in the Graph menu, you can take a look at your graph using the View option. Make sure you have a graph of six Bars before going any further. If you have not succeeded, then go back and repeat the process.

At this stage you should have a graph with a single Y variable which is identified as 'A' on the Graph menu. You now want to give the graph a title.

● Select Options from the Graph and from there Titles.

You will now have the four titles you require.

● For each of the titles enter:

First line:	XANIPAN INSURANCE BROKERS
Second line:	Premiums Collected - 1990
X-axis:	Brokers Office
Y-axis:	Premiums Collected

You can now inspect your graph from the Graph menu using View or from the spreadsheet using function key F10. At this stage you should have a bar chart similar to the one in Graph 8.1.

8.3 Multiple Bar Charts

The problem with the graph as it stands is that it fails to show all the information that is available in the spreadsheet. The totals show which brokers are the largest but the graph does not break down the size of business in each category as shown in the spreadsheet.

Look at graph 8.2 to see a graph which instead of showing the totals for each office shows the size of each category for each office.

There are, in fact, few differences between the two graphs. The titles are still the same and the X variable has not altered. One problem that has been taken away from you is the size of the scale. If you observe

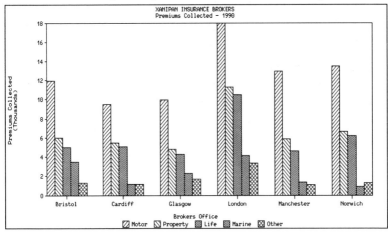

Graph 8.2

the Y-axis, you will see that the scale ranges from zero at the bottom to 18,000 at the top. In graph 8.1 the scale range was zero to 50,000. Lotus works all of this out for you.

Each City Broker is represented by six bars, one for each category of insurance. The bar for each insurance category is explained at the bottom of the screen by legends. This is an added extra you ought to put on your graph if an observer is to understand what is being shown.

The first step is to save the existing graph.

- From the Graph menu select the option sequence Name, Create and enter the 'Bar1'.

- Now reset 'A' which was the range showing the total premiums for each Office. This is done by selecting Reset from the Graph menu followed by 'A'.

- Now select 'A' from the Graph menu and give it the Range B8..B13. This represents the premiums from motor insurance.

Variable A will be shown on the Y-axis. All you need to do is to add in the other four bars for the remaining categories of insurance.

- In turn select the options B, C, D and E giving them the following ranges:

B	C8..C13
C	D8..D13
D	E8..E13
E	F8..F13

All that remains are the legends needed to identify what each bar represents.

- Select from Graph menu the command sequence Options, Legends. Enter for 'A' the legend 'Motor' and repeat for the other variables:

B	Property
C	Life
D	Marine
E	Other

On inspection of your graph, you should see the desired result.

● If you have colour, then from the \Graph menu select the command sequence Options, Colour to change the display to colour output.

8.4 Changing the perspective _____

You now have a graph that shows, for each office, the amount of premiums collected for each category of insurance. What if you want to show, for each category of insurance, how much each office collected? Graph 8.3 shows an example of this.

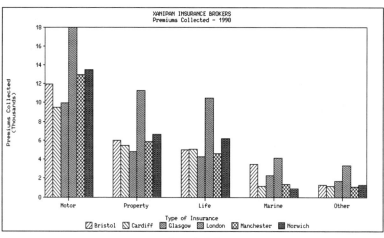

Graph 8.3

In this instance the X-axis variable is the category of insurance while the Y-axis variables are the six city offices. You can now see the relative importance of each category more clearly and how much each office has contributed to the total.

To achieve this perspective of the data you need to alter the X and Y variables as well as the legends. You will also have to change the title on the X-axis. The rest of the work has been done.

- From the Graph menu select the command sequence Name, Create and enter 'Bar2'. Print the graph if you want hard copy.

You now have two graphs named as part of this spreadsheet. The next job is to reset all the variables.

- From the Graph menu select Reset. Then select X to reset variable X and A to reset variable A and so on.

- Now set the X-axis by select X from the Graph menu and entering the range 'B6..F6' which are the categories of Insurance.

- For each of the other variables set them up as:

A	B8..F8
B	B9..F9
C	B10..F10
D	B11..F11
E	B12..F12
F	B13..F13

- From the Options in the Graph menu select Titles and enter a new title for the X-axis as 'Type of Insurance'.

- Finally, you need to alter the Legends which are in the Options menu as:

A	Bristol
B	Cardiff
C	Glasgow
D	London
E	Manchester
F	Norwich

- From the Graph menu select the command sequence Name, Create and enter the graph name 'Bar3'.

- Print the graph if you want a hard copy.

You now have a similar multiple bar chart with a different perspective.

8.5 Stacked bar chart _____

Looking at graph 8.3, you may not be satisfied that the reader can tell at a glance the size of each category of insurance. Observe the stacked bar chart in Graph 8.4.

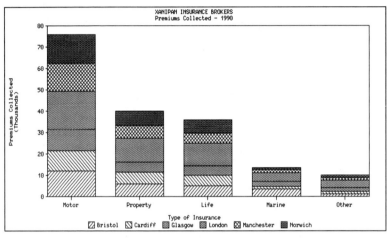

Graph 8.4

This graph uses one bar for each category on the X-axis while splitting up the bar into components for each of the Y variables. Again the scales have been drawn up for you.

● From the Graph menu select Type and choose the Stacked-Bar.

When you view the graph, everything has been done for you. Now do the same for the multiple graph that showed the amount of insurance premiums collected at each office.

● From the Graph menu select Name, Use and choose Bar2.

● From the Graph menu select Type and choose the Stacked-Bar.

When viewing this one, you can see the relative size of each office while at the same time you can see how the total premiums collected for each office are sub-divided. As you can see the process of going from multiple bars to stacked bars is a very simple and fast thing to do. Some people refer to the stacked bar charts as component bar charts.

8.6 The pie chart

In order to get a different view of the data, you can produce a pie chart that shows first the share of total premium contributions by office and then the share of total premium by their category. Graph 8.5 shows how each office has contributed to the total.

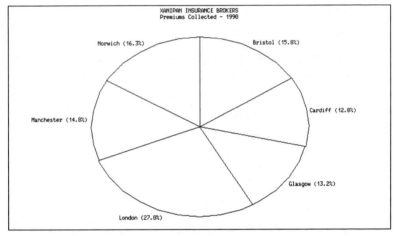

Graph 8.5

You can see at a glance the relative contribution each has made to the total.

In order to create a pie chart, a little less information is required than was needed for the bar charts. All you need is an X variable that is used to determine what each portion of the pie represents, an A variable to determine which figures to use and some titles at the top.

- From the Graph menu select the command sequence Reset, Graph.

- From the Graph menu select Type and choose the Pie Chart.

- Now set the X and A variables as:

X	A8..A13	for the offices
A	G8..G13	for the total premiums

- From the /Graph menu select Options and choose Titles entering the titles:

First line:	**XANIPAN INSURANCE BROKERS**
Second line:	Premiums Collected - 1990

On viewing your graph you should have the desired result.

- Name your graph as 'pie1'.

You can now alter the pie diagram to show the relative size of the types of insurance. In this instance, all that needs changing are the X and A variables.

- Reset your X and A variables.

- Set your new variables as:

X	B6..F6
A	G15..F15

- Name your graph as 'pie2'.

At this stage you will have a good number of named graphs that you can use at any time. You should now save your spreadsheet as a new example follows.

- From the main spreadsheet menu select File and Save and enter the file name 'graphs1'.

When the file is saved, it also saves the named graphs.

Before going on with the next section, your time would now be well spent calling up the different graphs, altering some of the numeric data on the spreadsheet to some of your own figures and viewing the differences that occur. Remember, Release 3 users have the added advantage of viewing a graph while at the same time being able to view and work on their spreadsheet. This is achieved by:

● Positioning the cursor somewhere in column E.

● Using the command sequence /Windows, Graph to see the graph appear on the right-hand side of the screen.

8.7 Line graphs

In this example a different spreadsheet is shown to compare a line graph with that of pie charts and bar charts. Begin by clearing your spreadsheet from the screen and making up a spreadsheet as shown in screen dump 8.2.

The spreadsheet shows the number of bottles of wine produced at a bottling plant over a ten year period. Along with the number of bottles for each year are the profits of the firm for that year.

● Start with a new spreadsheet and enter the details as shown in screen dump 8.2. There are no formulae or functions in this one

● From the Graph menu select Type and choose the Line graph.

You now need to determine the variables. As is normal, you want to see how things have changed over time. Consequently, you should use

```
A:C4: 'PROFITS                                                    READY

          A              B              C         D        E        F
1   WINE PRODUCTION FOR EURO DRINKS PLC
2
3
4   YEAR       NUMBER OF BOTTLES    PROFITS
5
6       1977              12000      10800
7       1978              13200      11000
8       1979              14500      13000
9       1980              16000      14000
10      1981              17900      14500
11      1982              21000      15000
12      1983              22900      15000
13      1984              25000      15000
14      1985              27500      15400
15      1986              30000       9000
16      1987              31500      -2000
17      1988              32000      -3000
18      1989              32000        600
19      1990              32100       5000
20
25-Oct-90   03:32 PM
```

Screen Dump 8.2

Time as the X-axis. As you want to see what has happened to production over time, select Numbers of Bottles as the Y variable.

● From the Graph menu select X and enter the range 'A6..A19'.

Now you need to enter some titles to put some meaning to the graph.

● From the Graph menu select Options and from here select Titles and enter the following:

First Line:	WINE PRODUCTION FOR EURO DRINKS PLC
X-axis:	NUMBER OF BOTTLES
Y-axis:	YEAR

Examine your graph and compare it with graph 8.6.

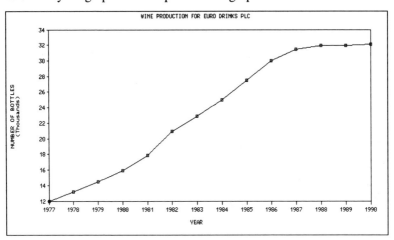

Graph 8.6

As with the bar charts, the scale has been worked out for you. You can see quite clearly that the volume of output has been growing since 1977.

If you want to enter your own scale to start, say, at zero on the Y axis and finish at 40, then you may do so. It can be achieved as follows:

- Select Options from the Graph menu and then choose Scale.

- From here choose Y-scale.

- Now choose Lower and enter '0' (zero) followed by Upper and enter '40'.

Go back and view your graph. Before going on any further, reset the scaling back to automatic.

- From the /Graph menu select the sequence of commands Options, Scale, Y-axis, Automatic.

We are now in a position to enter the details of profits obtained over the same period of time. Graph 8.7 shows you what you are trying to achieve.

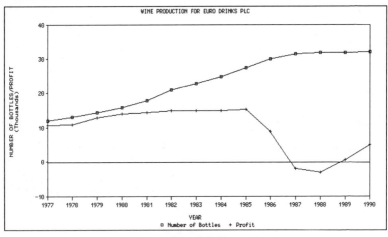

Graph 8.7

All you need to do is to create another variable, Profit, and enter legends for the two lines in order to inform an observer which one is which. You will also notice that the title on the Y-axis has been altered to indicate that there are two variables, Number of Bottles and Profit. Such a graph does give a very clear picture about what has happened to both output and profit and shows clearly when a loss was incurred; i.e. where the profit line has gone below the zero line.

- From the Graph menu select B and enter the range 'C6..C19'.

- Now select Options and choose Title from this in order to change the Y-axis title to 'NUMBER OF BOTTLES/PROFIT'.

- From Options you will also need to select Legends and give the following legends:

A	Number of Bottles
B	Profit

If your graph is to be used for accurate measures of profits and output at given times, then a grid might be of help. Try this out now.

- From the Graph menu select Options, Grid, Both and observe the outcome.

If you have Lotus release 3 and have a colour screen there is a way of defining what colours you want each line to be. Using the Options, Advanced, Colours you can select the different colours available to your machine.

8.8 Scatter graphs or XY graphs

Such graphs are used to show how one variable may, or may not, affect another. For example you will investigate whether in the example above there is any correlation between output and profit. In other words, does a higher output necessarily mean the firm will have a higher profit.

In such a case you need simply to plot one variable (X) against another variable (Y). Time does not matter in this case. Such a graph is depicted in graph 8.8.

It can be seen here that when profits are high it is not always the case that output is high. Such a graph, therefore plots one set of figures against another. To get to this kind of graph, you will find there is not as much work as with many other types of graph.

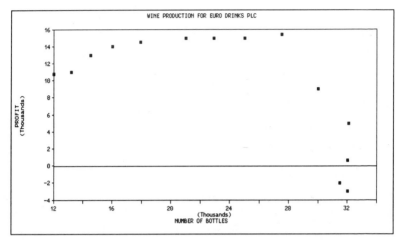

Graph 8.8

- From the Graph menu select Type and choose XY graph.

- Select X from the Graph menu and set it as the range B6..B19 and then select A and set this range as C6..C19.

- You will need to use Options to change the Legends. As they are no longer needed, rub them out for both X and A.

- Also within Options you will need to change two of the Titles:

X	NUMBER OF BOTTLES
A	PROFIT

- To avoid having the lines joined up select from the Graph menu the command sequence Options, Format, Graph, Symbols.

When observing your graph, you will see the changes. To get a better appreciation of this, experiment by altering some of the figures in both the Profit and Output columns. Try these:

1 Create numbers where it is obvious that higher output shows a higher profit.

2 Randomise the figures to show no pattern at all.

8.9 Summary _____

In this chapter you have:

- Determined an X-axis and Y-axis

- Set up a simple bar chart

- Constructed a multiple bar chart

- Entered titles and legends on to a graph

- Named and stored graphs

- Altered the perspective of a graph

- Constructed a stacked bar chart

- Constructed a pie chart

- Constructed line graphs with single and multiple lines

- Altered the scale of the axis of a graph

- Constructed a scatter graph (XY Graph)

9 FILES, MACROS AND PRINTING

9.1 Aims of this chapter

This chapter, as the title suggests, covers three main areas of activity. First it looks further at storing, retrieving and managing your spreadsheet and other files saved on disk. The second area will develop on the theme of macros which was introduced to you in chapter 7. Thirdly, it looks at further techniques of printing which will allow you to adapt your printing better to your output needs.

When working through this chapter, there are some sections that will only be of use to Lotus release 3 users.

Some of the principle objectives of manipulating file commands are:

● Saving worksheets, or parts of them

● Copying one worksheet into another

● Adding or subtracting the values of two worksheets

● Listing the names of files on disk

● Changing the data drive or directory

● Transferring data from other programs into a worksheet

Because much of this can be extremely demanding on someone less familiar with spreadsheets, it may be of benefit to set up some of these facilities as macros.

9.2 Filing

In Lotus 123 all work will be stored in files. Different files are used to store different types of information. The file types are distinguished by the three-character extension that is added as a suffix to them. The following file types are used:-

.wk3   to store worksheet (.wk1 for Release 3)
.prn   to store print formatted files
.pic   to store picture files generated from the graphics

Because release 3 does not need to use saved graph files for printing it does not need to use .pic files.

The File menu (/File) that appears has the following options:-

- Retrieve   Load a worksheet from the disk

- Save   Save a worksheet to disk

- Combine   Combine worksheets

- Xtract   Save a portion (range) of a worksheet

- Erase   Delete a file from disk

- List   List and identify an existing file

- Import   Bring files into Lotus 123 from other programs such as dBASE III and WordStar

- Directory   Change data drive or directory currently in use

As you have already looked at Retrieve and Save, the next section examines Combine.

9.3 Combining files

In order to give you some idea of the power of filing, this section will show you how more than one file can be combined in a way to accumulate sets of data. Examine screen dump 9.1.

The spreadsheet is a simple timesheet belonging to J SMITH. In rows 14 to 16 are formulae calculating the total pay.

- Enter the details of the spreadsheet. The cells that contain formulae are:

```
A:A1                                                           READY
A1: 'MONTHLY WORKSHEET FOR AN EMPLOYEE
J      A              B              C            D
1    MONTHLY_WORKSHEET FOR AN EMPLOYEE
2
3    EMPLOYEE NAME   J SMITH       HOURLY PAY RATE        6.00
4
5      WEEK NUMBER   BASIC HOURS  TIME-AND-A-HALF  DOUBLE
6
7             1          40            4            2
8             2          40            3            0
9             3          38            0            3
10            4          40            0            0
11
12                       HOURS         PAY
13
14   BASIC HOURS          158        948.00
15   TIME-AND-A-HALF        7         63.00
16   DOUBLE                 5         12.00
17
18             TOTAL GROSS PAY      1023.00
19
20
+
26-Oct-90  09:52 AM
```

Screen Dump 9.1

Cell	Formula	Cell	Formula
B14	@SUM(B6..B10)	C14	+B14*D3
B15	@SUM(C6..C10)	C15	+B15*D3*1.5
B16	@SUM(D6..D10)	C16	+B16*D3*2

The aim of this section is to find a way of accumulating the total wage bill that will comprise a number of such employees. To achieve this you will name the hours worked, create a new name and the use the command sequence File, Combine to add them together.

First you need to name a range. Although this is not essential to the objectives, it does make life a little easier.

- From the Lotus menu select Range followed by Name.

From screen dump 9.2 you can see that the Hours-Range has been named 'HOURS'.

- Name the range A7..D18 as 'HOURS'.

- Now save the spreadsheet with the command sequence the File, Save commands as file name 'SMITH'.

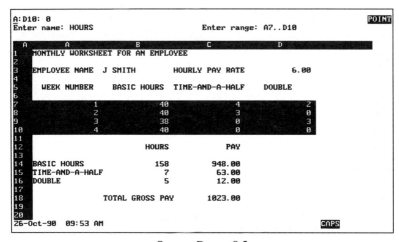

```
A:D10: 0                                              POINT
Enter name: HOURS              Enter range: A7..D10

   A          A            B              C            D
1  MONTHLY WORKSHEET FOR AN EMPLOYEE
2
3  EMPLOYEE NAME  J SMITH        HOURLY PAY RATE        6.00
4
5    WEEK NUMBER    BASIC HOURS  TIME-AND-A-HALF  DOUBLE
6
7               1           40            4            2
8               2           40            3            0
9               3           38            0            3
10              4           40            0            0
11
12                        HOURS          PAY
13
14 BASIC HOURS             158         948.00
15 TIME-AND-A-HALF           7          63.00
16 DOUBLE                    5          12.00
17
18              TOTAL GROSS PAY        1023.00
19
20
26-Oct-90  09:53 AM                                   CAPS
```

Screen Dump 9.2

Having done this, enter a new set of figures for another employee. In this case use the name 'JONES'.

● Change the figures as indicated in screen dump 9.3 and save the spreadsheet with the file name 'JONES'.

```
A:A2:                                                 READY

   A          A            B              C            D
1  MONTHLY WORKSHEET FOR AN EMPLOYEE
2
3  EMPLOYEE NAME  A JONES       HOURLY PAY RATE        6.00
4
5    WEEK NUMBER    BASIC HOURS  TIME-AND-A-HALF  DOUBLE
6
7               1           40            1            0
8               2           39            2            2
9               3           35            1            1
10              4           35            5            0
11
12                        HOURS          PAY
13
14 BASIC HOURS             149         894.00
15 TIME-AND-A-HALF           9          81.00
16 DOUBLE                    3          12.00
17
18              TOTAL GROSS PAY         987.00
19
20
26-Oct-90  09:53 AM                                   CAPS
```

Screen Dump 9.3

At this stage you have two files named 'JONES' and 'SMITH' and a set of corresponding data. In both cases the cell range A7..D18 has been named 'HOURS'.

● Generate a few more such timesheets remembering to save them with a different file name each time.

Now you are going to create a new summary spreadsheet. To do this erase all the hours. Leave the formula and text alone. All you need to clear for now is the Hours-Range and put something different where the name is.

● Use the command sequence Range, Erase from the Lotus menu and instead of entering a range to erase or pointing to what you want erased, simply enter 'HOURS'.

● In cell B3 enter 'Summary'.

Now you will combine the hours from the other files.

● Call the File menu and select Combine.

● The option you want is that of Add. Select this option and then choose Named/Specific Range.

● Enter the file name 'SMITH'.

● Now repeat these three stages and enter the file name 'JONES'.

● Repeat again for each of the names you entered.

Hopefully, you can now see what is happening. As each name is added so the totals accumulate. Subtracting is just as easy. Instead of replying Add to Combine, you enter Subtract.

Combine allows you the three options

● Overlay ALL or part of the worksheet with values

● Add values

● Subtract values

Copying one worksheet into another _____

The command sequence File, Combine, Copy is used to copy data from diskette INTO the current worksheet. This is called linking worksheets. You must position the cell pointer where you want the file to be copied into before using this command.

Consider using the command to:

1 Complete a worksheet with labels, values or formulae from disk file.

2 Add one or more sets of macro instructions to the current worksheets.

9.4 Saving parts of a worksheet _____

The command sequence /File, Extract, Save saves part of a worksheet and is useful when

1 A worksheet is too large to store on one disk. This will require you to specify a range to save rather than a whole spreadsheet.

2 You want to save key parts to be combined with another worksheet later.

3 You want to create a library of often used entries or operations or something that is particularly tricky.

9.5 Managing file storage _____

There are a number of commands to help tell you which files are stored and where and how to bring in files from other programs.

• The command sequence File, List displays all file names stored on disk and how much disk space is left. This is particularly useful to find a file for which you have forgotten the name.

• The command sequence File, Erase deletes unwanted files. You will be required to give the file name and type. You will also be required to confirm this action, which is designed to guard against accidental erasure.

- The command sequence File, Directory is used to change either the disk drive or directory in use, or both. For the sake of good file management, you will want to keep various sets of files to specific directories.

The command sequence File, Import copies files in ASCII format, such as those created by word processing packages and BASIC programs, into a specified worksheet location.

Screen dump 9.4 is an example of the kind of response you might get to the file sequence of commands File, List.

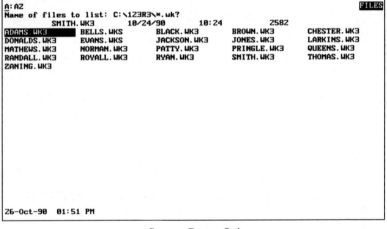

Screen Dump 9.4

/File, Import steps are:

- Give the file a '.prn' extension.

- Position the cell pointer to a place where you want to import the data.

- Check that the data disk is in the drive.

- Select /File, Import and for the data types:

Text – each line of the import file is a separate left justified label in a separate worksheet row, i.e. a column of long labels.

Numbers – imports numbers as values and text in double quotation marks as text with other file contents being ignored. Each number and line of valid text will be placed in a separate cell and a separate row.

The use of this file command is to allow you to enter into a spreadsheet data that has been generated by another applications package such as a word processor, database, accounts or even another spreadsheet.

9.6 **More on macros**

This second section will take advantage of some macros as a way of making some of the filing commands much easier to initiate. Later on, you will be shown other applications of macros.

In chapter 4 you arrived at a spreadsheet that showed the sales analysis of Lotus Motor Sales. Using this spreadsheet model the use of some macros can be demonstrated on the spreadsheet model set out in screen dump 9.5.

```
A: A1: [W20]                                                    READY

      A           A          B           C           D           E
                                    Lotus Motor Sales
 1                                  Motor sales for January
 2
 3
 4                             Mini Van    Saloon    Hatch Back Estate
 5
 6    Net Price                7800.00     6900.00    7750.00    8600.00
 7    VAT (15%)                1170.00     1035.00    1162.50    1290.00
 8    Gross Price              8970.00     7935.00    8912.50    9890.00
 9    Registration Cost          60.00       60.00      60.00      60.00
10    Sale Price               9030.00     7995.00    8972.50    9950.00
11
12    Number of sales             18          33         37         28
13    Total Income           162540.00   263835.00  331982.50  278600.00
14
15    Grand Total Income    1036957.50
16    Unit Sales                 116
17    Average Sale Price        8939.29
18    Number of models             5
19    Most sold                   37
20    Least sold                  18
20-Oct-90   09:23 AM
```

Screen Dump 9.5

If you followed the advice on saving the file in chapter 4, then it will have the name motors.

- Use the file operation to retrieve this spreadsheet. If you do not have the file on hand, then you will need to return to chapter 4 and generate a new one.

Begin by entering a macro that will print out the spreadsheet. In order to print the spreadsheet you might find it worthwhile entering the following key strokes:

/PPRA1..F2~GQ

- Go to cell A23 and enter this macro as a cell label remembering that an apostrophe (') is needed at the beginning to indicate that it is a label.

- Using the command sequence Range, Name and Create label the range A23..A23 with the name '\P'.

Having done this, pressing the keys ALT and P simultaneously will perform the necessary commands to print your spreadsheet. This should demonstrate the purpose of a macro, to simplify a series of operations by recording them in a cell and then activating them with one key stroke.

- Enter a macro that will save your spreadsheet automatically. The macro is:

\FSLSM~R

- Name this macro as 'S' and store it in cell B24.

- Activate this macro to be sure that it works.

- Now enter the a macro into cell A25 that will quit from the spreadsheet. The macro is:

\QY

Do not try running this macro until you have saved your spreadsheet again.

Now for something much more ambitious! You will write a routine that will collect a new set of monthly sales figures and automatically display them as graphs. The principle is fairly straightforward; you will need to enter a list of commands and name a range of cells as the macro. the following cell entries are an example of how to achieve this:

A27:	{goto}b12~ A28: {?}~
A29:	{goto}c12~
A30:	{?}~
A31:	{goto}d12~
A32:	{?}~
A33:	{goto}e12~
A34:	{?}~
A35:	{goto}f12~
A36:	{?}~
A37:	{graph}

The use of the curly brackets {—} is to issue a command that is not contained in the menu structure. The 'goto' command is an instruction to go to a cell (the cell location follows) and the question mark, ?, is to indicate that an operator will need to make an entry followed by pressing the Return key before carrying on.

In summary then, the list will go to a cell where the sales figure appear and collect a new sales value.

This is carried out for the sales of each model of car.

At cell A37 above, the command instructs that a graph should be shown, depicting the new pattern of cells.

- Enter the above macro into the respective cells.

- Using the command sequence Range, Name and Create label the range A27..A37 with the name '\C'.

- Now experiment with this macro and try to follow exactly what is happening.

You should begin to appreciate that the capabilities of macros are enormous, and it is beyond the scope of this book to cover all possibilities. When constructing a macro of this dimension, you are in fact undergoing a computer programming exercise. Although programming is very much a well developed skill in its own right requiring a good deal of training and experience, some of the simplest programs can be very effective and are within the capabilities of a non-programmer.

It is always worthwhile producing, for the benefit of an operator, some advice on the macros that are available. To demonstrate this, attempt the following procedure.

- Enter the text that appears in screen dump 9.6 into the respective cells of your spreadsheet:

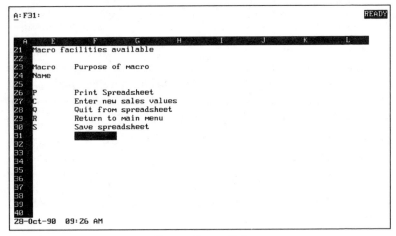

Screen Dump 9.6

On the basis of this, you will need to create two new macros. One macro is required to go to cell A1 and the other to go to cell E21 which is the location of this help screen. Try this yourself as a challenge.

9.7 More on printing

One of the first possibilities that should be explained is the use of a print file on a disk which can be distinguished by the file extension '.prn'.

Such a print file can be created by a spreadsheet when you want to delay printing for a later date. Some possible reasons for this might be:

- You have no printer available at the present moment.

- You have to use a network printer which is currently being used by someone else or you have been allotted specific times for its use which do not include the time you want to use your spreadsheet.

- You want to store the printing in a file, take it to another machine with a better printer and print it from there.

- You want to save all your printing and batch process them all off at once rather than one at a time.

However, often a more probable reason is the fact that the file created is in a form that can be read by another program, in particular a word processing package. This facility is extremely useful when you want your spreadsheet incorporated into a report.

Whatever your reason, the technique is relatively simple. To create a print file you do the following:

- Select the command sequence /Print, File. When you simply wanted to use the printer you used the command sequence /Print, Printer.

- You will then be asked for a file name. Enter a file name with no more than eight characters and with spaces. The file extension of '.prn' will be added to the file name for you.

- Carry on as though you were printing. All output is directed to the file and not to the printer.

When you want to print the file, the operating system cop command will be able to send the file to the printer. If the file is to be read by another program, you will need to examine that other program to determine how the file is read in.

9.8 Examining cell contents

Another very useful feature of Lotus, is being able to see the contents of your file. If you examine screen dump 9.7 you will see that it displays what is actually in the cells such as text, numbers, formulae and functions.

```
A: A1: [W20]                                                        READY

      A              A            B          C         D         E
1                                          Lotus Motor Sales
2                                          Motor sales for January
3
4                              Mini Van      Saloon   Hatch Back Estate
5
6   Net Price                      7800        6900       7750      8600
7   VAT (15%)                    +B6*0.15   +C6*0.15  +D6*0.15  +E6*0.15
8   Gross Price                  +B6+B7     +C6+C7    +D6+D7    +E6+E7
9   Registration Cost               60          60        60        60
10  Sale Price                   +B8+B9     +C8+C9    +D8+D9    +E8+E9
11
12  Number of sales                 18          33        37        28
13  Total Income                 +B10*B12   +C10*C12  +D10*D12  +E10*E12
14
15  Grand Total Income  @SUM(B13..F13)
16  Unit Sales                    116
17  Average Sale Price  +B15/@SUM(B12..F12)
18  Number of models                5
19  Most sold                      37
20  Least sold                     18
20-Oct-90  09:28 PM
```

Screen Dump 9.7

Try this out now.

- Retrieve the file 'motors'.

- From the Worksheet menu select Global then Format.

- Select Text to convert the cell to show formulae and functions.

- Now widen the cells enough to see the entire cell contents.

To reverse this process, you will need to repeat the stages above. In practice, because all the cells have been altered to cater for the new perspective of the spreadsheet, it is probably quicker to Retrieve the original file.

However, you will probably want a printout of the cell contents rather than see it on-screen. This allows you to have all the cell contents visible at the same time and allows you to take the information away for inspection at your own leisure.

● From the Print menu select Printer followed by Options.

● Now you want to choose Other which gives you more choices.

As-displayed: This prints the display screen. This is the default for the system.

Cell-for-mulas: This prints the actual contents of every cell in sequence down your page on the printer.

Formatted: This prints all the headers, footers and page breaks that you and your printer have defined. A header appears at the top of the screen and is text set up in the Options, Borders selected from Print. A Footer is exactly the same but appears below the spreadsheet.

Unformatted: This leaves out any headers, footers and page breaks.

● Select As-displayed and using ESC return to the main Print menu.

● Select Align which ensures you start at the top of the page, in other words a page break will not appear too soon into printing.

● Make sure the paper in your printer is aligned and select Go.

To ensure that you print the spreadsheet as displayed in the future, you will need to go back and reverse the process with Printer, Option, Other and then As-displayed. The settings are not forgotten once set.

This process whereby when you select an option, it sets a condition and to reset it you reverse the process, is often called a **toggle**.

9.9 Summary

Throughout this chapter some of the extended features of the Lotus package have been demonstrated. As you will no doubt appreciate, there is far more to the Lotus package than is possible to introduce in this book. A good deal of knowledge will come from continued practice.

Most users will have their special requirements of such a package and will tend to get to know certain capabilities of the package very well while virtually ignoring many other features. This approach is quite normal with almost any package.

In this chapter you have:

- Established further objectives of file handling

- Used File, Combine to add data ranges and subtract data ranges from one spreadsheet into another

- Described file management activities of directory listings, erasing files and determining in which directories to place files

- Developed further macros, in particular a sequence of macro instructions in the form of a computer program

- Output spreadsheet to print files for future printing or for entering into other packages

- Displayed and printed cell contents

10 THREE DIMENSIONAL SPREADSHEETS

10.1 Aims of this chapter

This chapter will introduce you to the idea of working with multiple Sheets. Lotus refers to the concept as '3-D' or three dimensional.

The principle is that a spreadsheet has columns and rows and so is two-dimensional and a third dimension is introduced by having LAYERS of Sheets one on top of the other. Lotus allows you to have up to 256 such Sheets making up a spreadsheet. It works rather like a book in that each page reads across and down while a whole series of pages make up the book. In fact, throughout this chapter, each page, or two dimensional spreadsheet, will be referred to as a **Sheet** while the collection of these Sheets will be referred to as the Spreadsheet.

10.2 Looking at multiple Sheets

- Enter 123 so that a blank Sheet is displayed on your screen.

- Select /Window from the 123 menu and from here Window.

- Now select Perspective.

At this stage you will see three Sheets on your screen similar to those shown in screen dump 10.1.

The one in the front is labelled as Sheet 'A' and is the only active Sheet in the spreadsheet. This chapter will require you to work with four Sheets to show you how 123 works with multiple Sheets.

From the menu:

- Select Worksheet, Insert, Sheet and After. You will now be asked how many Sheets you want to insert. Respond with entering the number 4.

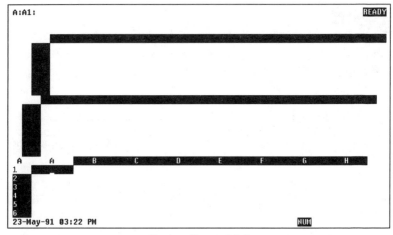

Screen Dump 10.1

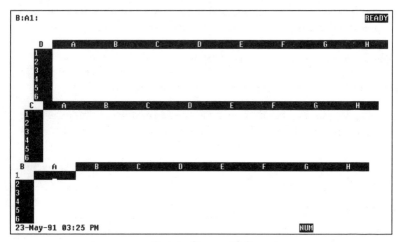

Screen Dump 10.2

Screen dump 10.2 shows that Sheets B, C and D are displayed at the same time. As you will observe, they are all labelled with row numbers and column letters. The perspective view of the spreadsheet shows exactly three Sheets at any one time, Sheet 'A' has not been lost.

Although you have selected four Sheets you will see later in this chapter that you can always add Sheets or insert new ones between existing ones, rather like adding or inserting new pages into a loose leaf book.

The cursor should be highlighted in cell A1 of Sheet 'B'. From the top left-hand indicator in the screen you will see that this cell location is B:A1.

● Press the Ctrl and Page Up keys simultaneously to move up to Sheet 'C'.

● Now use the Ctrl and Page Down keys simultaneously to move back to Sheet 'B'.

● Use Ctrl and Page Down again to reveal Sheet 'A'. You will observe that Sheet 'D' has now left the screen.

Within each Sheet the right, left, up and down arrow keys are used to move within a Sheet. Experiment further with moving between Sheets and within Sheets until you are familiar with the idea.

You should now be able to see what is meant by the concept of a three dimensional spreadsheet. We now have Columns with letter headings A,B,C,D..., Rows with numbers 1,2,3,4,5... and layers of Sheets A:,B:,C... . The next stage is to see what can be done with this extra dimension.

10.3 Setting up the first Sheet

This example will begin by setting up Sheet 'A' with a Sales Analysis table for sales of products by a company to different countries in the month of October. When building up any single Sheet, working with PERSPECTIVE mode will prove awkward because of only being able to view six lines in a Sheet; so we will clear this when making up a Sheet.

- Using the Ctrl and Page Up keys or Ctrl and Page Down keys make sure the cursor is within Sheet 'A'. This sets the current Sheet as 'A'.

- Now clear the perspective using the command sequence /Worksheet, Window, Clear.

Although you will only see one Sheet in the conventional two-dimensioned way, Sheets B, C and D are still resident. It will be rather like having a book open and only being able to see the current page you are looking at; the others are still there.

- As a first measure, widen the column widths to 20 using the command sequence /Worksheet, Global, Column, Set-Width, 20.

- Enter the label 'EUROPA COMPONENTS' in cell A1 and 'Sales Analysis by Country – OCTOBER 1990' in cell A3.

Observe screen dump 10.3.

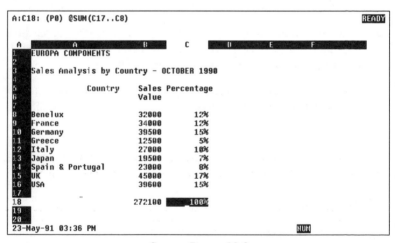

Screen Dump 10.3

- Enter the column headings: 'Country' in cell A5, 'Sales' in cell B5, 'Percentage' in cell C5 and 'Value' in cell B6.

- To make the headings more presentable, right justify the labels using the command sequence /Range, Labels Right selecting the range A5..C6.

- Enter each of the country names shown in Screen Dump 10.3 starting with 'Benelux' in cell A8. Then enter the sales values for each country starting with 32000 in cell B8.

- Enter the function @SUM(B8..B16) in cell B18 to give total sales for the month.

- The formula in cell C8 is +B8/$B$18. Enter this and use the 123 copy facility to copy the formula from cell B8..B8 to B9..B16. Having done this, format the range for percentage display using the command sequence /Range, Format, Percent and entering the range C8..C16.

Entering the formula into cell C8 with the dollar ($) sign was important because you needed the absolute cell location of B18 to form the formula throughout the column cells when copying it.

- Enter the function @SUM(C8..C16) in cell C18 to give total percentage for the month. You will then need to format this cell to percentage display to give 100%.

- Now set the display to Perspective with the command sequence /Worksheet, Window, Perspective.

Examine screen dump 10.4 and compare it with your own.

You will notice that only six lines of Sheet 'A' show at any time, which poses problems when you are working with the spreadsheet.

10.4 Copying between sheets

Our next objective is to copy the entire 'A' Sheet into the 'B' Sheet. The principle here is no different to copying from one range of cells to another.

- Make sure your current Sheet is 'A'; i.e. the cursor is in Sheet 'A'.

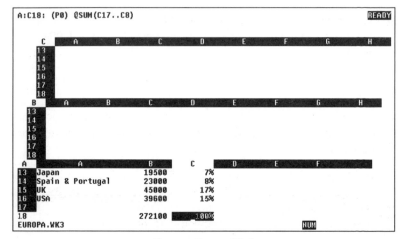

Screen Dump 10.4

- From the main command menu select /Copy and either highlight the range A1..C18 or enter the range in.

- Now use the Ctrl and Page Up keys to jump to Sheet 'B'.

- Move the cursor to cell B1 in this Sheet and press ENTER.

The end result of this was to Copy from A:A1..C8 to B:A1. You now have an identical copy of the Sheets in both parts of the spreadsheet. However, you have a problem, because the two Sheets have different column widths, the data will not fit into their cells correctly in Sheet 'B'. To solve this, you can do one of two things:

1 Alter the columns in Sheet 'B' to be compatible with that of Sheet 'A'.

2 Use the Lotus GROUP facility to make sure that formats are the same throughout all Sheets in the spreadsheet.

- To set all Sheets with the same format use the command sequence /Worksheet, Global, Group, Enable.

This solves the immediate problem.

10.5 Entering three-dimensional formulae _____

- Making sure you are positioned in the 'B' Sheet, remove the perspective with the command sequence /Worksheet, Window, Clear.

- Examine screen dump 10.5 and make the necessary alterations to the label in cell A3 and the individual sales values for the countries. The rest of the Sheet will take care of itself.

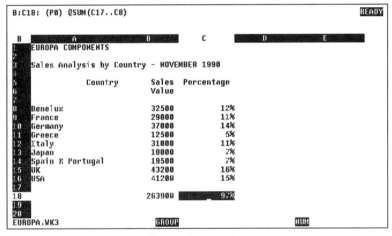

Screen Dump 10.5

You will now enter into Sheet 'B' a formula that works out the difference between sales in the current month of November with the sales of the previous month of October.

- First of all set the column widths to 12 using the command sequence /Worksheet, Global, Col-width, Set-Width, 12.

- Enter the new column headings of 'Sales change' in cell D5 and 'on month' in cell D6.

Now you are ready to use a formula that links with the other Sheet.

- In cell D8 enter the formula +B8-A:B8.

Cell B8 contains the monthly sales for Benelux in the current Sheet for November. Cell A:B8 is in Sheet 'A' and contains the Benelux sales in that Sheet which is for October. The result was to find the difference in sales between the two months. A negative figure would have meant a fall in sales while a positive figure would mean a rise in sales.

Now you will need to do the same for the remaining countries. Because the relative positioning of the cells in the 'A' Sheet are the same, the Copy command can be used.

- Select /Copy and copy FROM D8..D8 which is the cell with the formula in it TO D9..D16.

- Now enter the totalling function in cell D18 of @SUM(D8..D16). You can also achieve the same result by comparing the two monthly totals with the formula +B18-A:B18.

Screen dump 10.6 shows the resulting Sheet 'B'.

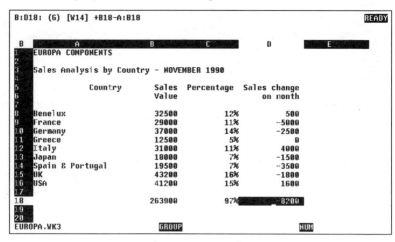

Screen Dump 10.6

10.6 Building up a history

The next task is to copy all data from Sheet 'B' to Sheet 'C' to give sales for December.

- Restore the perspective with /Worksheet, Window, Perspective and make sure the current Sheet is 'B'.

- Now use Copy and highlight the range to copy From as A1..D18. To copy TO use the keys Ctrl and Page Up to jump to Sheet 'C'. Move to cell A1 in this Sheet and then press ENTER.

Screen dump 10.7 shows the result.

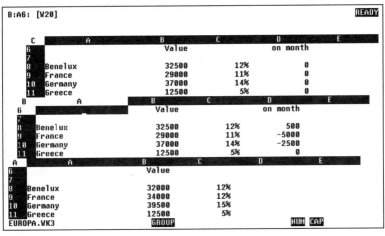

Screen Dump 10.7

You will notice that the 'Sales Change on Month' column shows all zeros. This is exactly to be expected because there has been no change over the two months as all the sales figures are the same. This would confirm that the formulae have been copied successfully as well as numbers and labels.

- Alter the label cell A3 to indicate that we are entering sales for December and not November.

• Using the data shown in screen dump 10.8, alter the sales figures for the countries and observe what happens to the figures in the column 'Sales Changes over the month' as you work through it.

```
C:A1: [W20] 'EUROPA COMPONENTS                                    READY

  C          A              B         C          D              E
1   EUROPA COMPONENTS
2
3  Sales Analysis by Country - DECEMBER 1990
4
5                    Country      Sales  Percentage  Sales change
6                                 Value              on month
7
8  Benelux                        31900      12%         -600
9  France                         29800      11%          800
10 Germany                        36500      13%         -500
11 Greece                         22000       8%         9500
12 Italy                          31200      11%          200
13 Japan                          17600       6%         -400
14 Spain & Portugal               20000       7%          500
15 UK                             41500      15%        -1700
16 USA                            41600      15%          400
17
18                               272100     100%         8200
19
20
EUROPA.WK3                       GROUP                    NUM CAP
```

Screen Dump 10.8

You should now appreciate that the task becomes easier as we work through the months. You may, for example, want to go on with this for many months.

10.7 Summarising the sheets _____

The next task is to produce a summary Sheet that adds all the monthly sales together. You could enter this as, say, Sheet 'Z' giving us room to insert more months after December. However, this is unnecessary as you will always have the opportunity of inserting Sheets between existing ones in the same way as you can insert new lines into a single Sheet.

Screen dump 10.9 shows the desired result where the Sales Value figures are the totals for the three months on Sheets A, B and C.

• Copy the contents of Sheet 'C' Range A1..C18 into Sheet 'D' and adjust the label in A3 as shown in Screen dump 10.9.

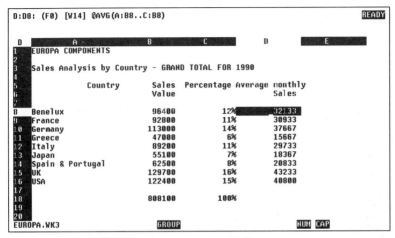

Screen Dump 10.9

- Remove the Perspective and make sure the current cell is Sheet 'D'.

- Now enter the formula @SUM(A:B8..C:B8) into cell B8.

- Copy the function in cell B8 From B8..B8 To B9..B16 and you will have achieved the desired result.

The function in cell B8 has added together the contents of A:B8, B:B8 and C:B8 in a three-dimensional sense. It would now be easy to add another month by month between Sheets 'C' and 'D' and still maintain the summary Sheet. By simply making sure you are in Sheet 'D' the command /Worksheet, Insert, Sheet, Before would have the desired effect.

We suggest that you try something like this in an attempt to get a good understanding of what multiple or three-dimensional spreadsheets are about.

Another demonstration of the usefulness of multiple Sheets will be shown by taking average monthly sales of the period.

- Go to the Sheet where the summary totals are kept and enter into cell D5 the label 'Average Monthly' and in cell D6 the label 'Sales'.

- Enter into cell C8 a function that calculates the average. The function @AVG(A:B8..C:B8) will calculate the average for three months, but you may have to change C:B8 in the function if you have added in extra Sheets.

10.8 Versatile graphs

As a final demonstration on the versatility of multiple Sheets observe screen dump 10.10.

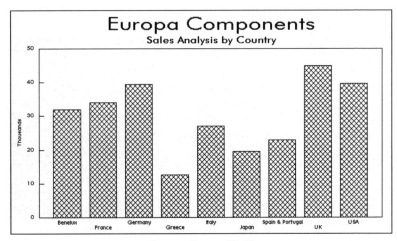

Screen Dump 10.10

The graph is a bar chart of sales for each country in the first month that was set up in Sheet 'A' for October 1990. Do this by:

- Going Sheet 'A' and select from the /Graph menu Type followed by Bar.

- Select X from this menu and set the range for as the 'Country Names' which is the range A8..A16. Then choose the A Range as B8..B16.

- From the /Graph, Options menu select Titles, First and enter the name 'Europa Components' and Options, Title, Second as 'Sales Analysis by Country'.

Now view the graph and you will see the plotted data for Sheet 'A'.

- Return to the spreadsheet and go to the Sheet you have used to summarise the sales. Use the key marked F10 on your keyboard to examine the graph again.

The graph you get should look something like the one in screen dump 10.11.

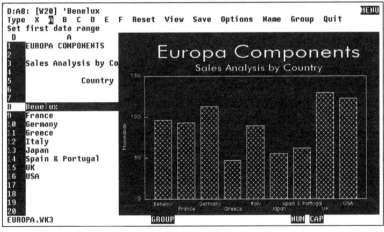

Screen Dump 10.11

The data plotted by the graph will always be the one in the current Sheet. If you wanted to save a particular graph for subsequent printing, then using the Command Sequence /Graph, Save will allow this so that you can save a series of graphs for the months without having to keep jumping to different Sheets.

The ability Lotus has to redraw graphs to match changing data in Sheets really comes to life when you see a graph in a window and move through the Sheets.

- Move to Sheet 'A' making sure that that is the only Sheet visible on the screen.

- Use the command sequence /Worksheet, Window, Graph to see the current graph.

- Now move through the Sheet to see the effect.

10.9 Chapter Summary

In this chapter, you have:

- Viewed and moved between multiple Sheets of a spreadsheet.

- Entered data into one Sheet and copied it into another.

- Entered formulae and functions into a Sheet that are derived from other Sheets.

- Set up a graph that has the versatility to change itself to suit the parameters of the current Sheet.

SAMPLE EXERCISES

11.1 Aims of this chapter

This book has introduced you to a large variety of applications of spreadsheets. This chapter offers further ideas for spreadsheet use.

In addition some exercises will help develop your skills further with the Lotus package. If you work through the exercises in sequence, you will find that they are graded in such a way that they become more demanding as you work through them.

11.2 Selling soft toys

1 Load up your spreadsheet and give the spreadsheet the title 'EXPENSE DETAILS FOR HARRY'S SOFT TOYS' on the first row. On the third row enter the author's name (your name) along with the date it was generated.

2 Entering the current date can be done by entering a cell function @TODAY. This will generate a number which will need to be formatted. This is done by using the command sequence /Range, Format, Date and then highlight the 'DD-MMM-YY' option followed by pressing the Return key twice.

3 Enter the spreadsheet shown in screen dump 11.1.

4 Incorrect information has been collected on the costs of sundries which should be 60 in February and 50 in April. Adjust the amounts accordingly to recalculate the total costs.

5 Create two new columns for May and June and copy the data in February across to May and the data January into June.

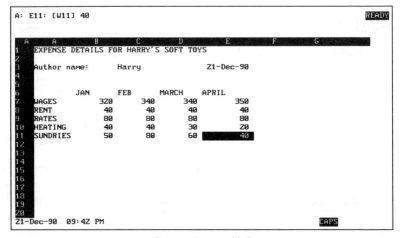

Screen Dump 11.1

6 Generate the total costs for each of the months, using the @SUM function. Give it a row title of 'TOTAL COST'.

7 Print out the entire spreadsheet and save the file with the name 'SHOP-A'.

8 Increase all the columns by 2 characters and format the numbers to 2 decimal places.

9 Add a new row at the end of the spreadsheet and give it a title of 'SALES INCOME' followed by, for each month, the following sales income values:

	JAN	FEB	MARCH	APRIL	MAY	JUNE
SALES INCOME	2000	3000	3000	4000	5000	5000

10 Now add a final row called 'SURPLUS' and under the JAN column enter a formula that shows the surplus value as being:

(SALES INCOME) – (TOTAL COST).

11.3 Arnold's fish bar

1 Load up your spreadsheet package and enter your name and today's date at the top of the spreadsheet.

2 Enter a title on row 3 called 'ARNOLD'S FISH BAR SALES'.

3 Set up the spreadsheet with the labels shown in screen dump 11. 2 with the column headings starting on row 5 and the row headings in column A.

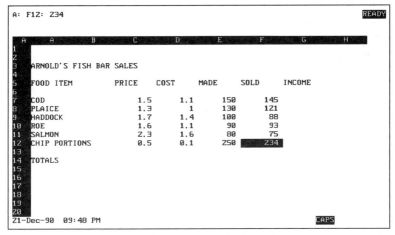

Screen Dump 11.2

4 The numbers that appear in the spreadsheet should also be entered. Make sure that your text is left justified and your numbers are right justified. This should confirm that you have entered them correctly.

5 Generate the INCOME obtained from COD by multiplying the PRICE by the number SOLD, putting the answer in the INCOME column. Use the Lotus Copy facility to copy this formula to calculate the income made from each item.

6 Use a formula to calculate the total items MADE, the total dishes SOLD and the total INCOME.

7 Add an extra column to the spreadsheet to show the profit made on each dish. Under the heading PROFIT generate the data for each dish using the formula:

PROFIT = INCOME - (COST * MADE).

Total this column to calculate the overall profit for all the dishes, putting the answers on the TOTALS row.

8 Now change the numeric data to the ones shown in screen dump 11.3b to check that your spreadsheet still calculates the INCOME, PROFIT and TOTALS correctly with the new figures.

9 Finally, produce two more columns with column headings 'UNSOLD' to hold the amount of stock for each item that was left unsold (MADE - SOLD) and a column headed 'WASTE' to hold the cost to the fish bar of this unsold stock (UNSOLD * COST). Compare the outcome with that shown in screen dump 11.3.

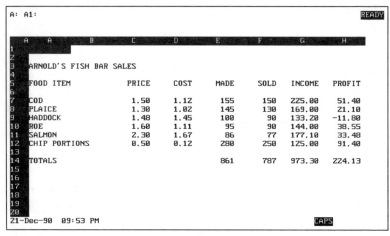

Screen Dump 11.3

11.4 Electricity bill

This exercise requires you to set up a model electricity bill similar to that shown in screen dump 11.4.

```
A: A1:                                                              READY

    A        B          C          D          E        F        G        H
 1                        EUROPA ELECTRICITY BOARD PLC
 2
 3   Customer Name:    Mr J Smith
 4   Customer Address: 1 Low Street
 5                     St Monty's Sq.
 6
 7   Current Meter     Last Meter       No. of            Standard
 8   Reading           Reading          Units             Charge
 9
10      9606              7736            1870               8.28
11
12
13            Cost Per Unit:             5.94 pence
14
15            Total Cost for Units:     111.08
16            Standing Charge             8.28
17
18                TOTAL NOW DUE:        119.36
19
20
    21-Dec-90   09:59 PM
```

Screen Dump 11.4

When you set out this spreadsheet, bear in mind the following formulae:

No. of Units = (Current Meter Reading) - (Last Meter Reading)

Total Cost for Units = (No. of Units) * (Cost per Unit)

TOTAL NOW DUE = (Total Cost for Units) + (Standard Charge)

When you complete this exercise, experiment with a few bills with different meter readings to convince yourself that the spreadsheet works correctly.

11.5 Calorie control

The following exercise is an example of how a spreadsheet can be used to give instant and accurate measures of the number of calories contained within a specific diet. It is the kind of application for which a spreadsheet can be used, and you will no doubt be able to think of many more such applications as you work through this one.

The spreadsheet is split up into two parts: one part contains the ACTUAL DIET of a given patient, while the second part contains the CALORIE CONTROL CHART. Release 3 users will place the calorie control chart in sheet 'B' and the actual diet details in sheet 'A'. Basically, the spreadsheet will collect the details of the patient from a user, and then calculate the calories consumed in the diet by reading these details from Calorie Control Chart.

Calorie control chart

The chart will need to go somewhere on the spreadsheet where it is out of the way, as this data will be standard and does not need to be changed too often.

1   Start at position K1 if you are release 2 user or A1 in Sheet B if you are a Release 3 user and enter the following chart details:

Screen dump 11.5   shows the calorie value for 100 gram.

```
B: A1: [W22] 'CALORIE CONTROL CHART - Figures are Calorie measure          READY

   B         A              B       C        D              E
1   CALORIE CONTROL CHART - Figures are Calorie measure
2
3   Breafast Cereal        460           Milk - Skimmed        35
4   Chocolate              600           Milk - Full Crem      70
5   Ice Cream              180           Wine                  74
6   Jam                    300           Yoghurt - Normal     175
7   Digestive Biscuit       80           Yoghurt - Low Fat    125
8   Chocolate Digestive     85           Yoghurt - Diet        85
9   Bread (4 slices)       260           Apple - Med           50
10  Butter                 840           Banana                80
11  Low Fat Spread         420           Orange                60
12  Pasta                  420           Peach                 35
13  Peanuts                640
14  Potatoes - Chips       280           The measure is expressed
15            Roast        100           per 100 grammes (g) or per
16            Boiled       185           100 millilitres
17
18  All vegetable, other than potatoes and peas are of minimum significance
19
20
21-Dec-90  10:08 PM
```

Screen Dump 11.5

When generating this table, you will need to adjust the column width sizes.

2   Print out this chart only. You will need to specify the range you wanted printed prior to its printing.

Patient diet sheet

3 Now enter a patient diet sheet for a given day, starting at position A1 to look something like the data in screen dumps 11.6 and 11.7 . Release 3 users will need to move to Sheet 'A' for this.

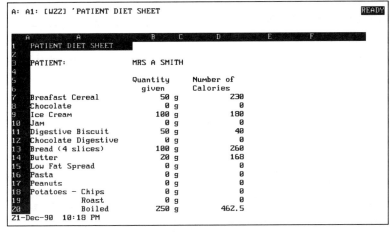

```
A: A1: [W22] 'PATIENT DIET SHEET                                    READY

   A          A            B      C       D         E        F
1  PATIENT DIET SHEET
2
3  PATIENT:               MRS A SMITH
4
5                         Quantity      Number of
6                         given         Calories
7  Breafast Cereal          50 g            230
8  Chocolate                 0 g              0
9  Ice Cream               100 g            180
10 Jam                       0 g              0
11 Digestive Biscuit        50 g             40
12 Chocolate Digestive       0 g              0
13 Bread (4 slices)        100 g            260
14 Butter                   20 g            168
15 Low Fat Spread            0 g              0
16 Pasta                     0 g              0
17 Peanuts                   0 g              0
18 Potatoes - Chips          0 g              0
19           Roast           0 g              0
20           Boiled        250 g            462.5
21-Dec-90  10:18 PM
```

Screen Dump 11 .6

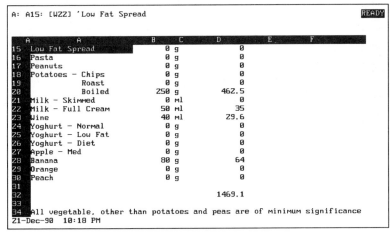

```
A: A15: [W22] 'Low Fat Spread                                       READY

   A          A            B      C       D         E        F
15 Low Fat Spread            0 g              0
16 Pasta                     0 g              0
17 Peanuts                   0 g              0
18 Potatoes - Chips          0 g              0
19           Roast           0 g              0
20           Boiled        250 g            462.5
21 Milk - Skimmed            0 ml             0
22 Milk - Full Cream        50 ml            35
23 Wine                     40 ml            29.6
24 Yoghurt - Normal          0 g              0
25 Yoghurt - Low Fat         0 g              0
26 Yoghurt - Diet            0 g              0
27 Apple - Med               0 g              0
28 Banana                   80 g             64
29 Orange                    0 g              0
30 Peach                     0 g              0
31
32                                         1469.1
33
34 All vegetable, other than potatoes and peas are of minimum significance
21-Dec-90  10:18 PM
```

Screen Dump 11 .7

4 Make sure that the entries of the NUMBER OF CALORIES are found and calculated by the computer. For example the number of calories for Milk – Full Cream in cell number D22 is calculated as follows:

Grams given found in cell B22 divided by 100 and then multiplied by the number of calories per 100 millilitres which was placed into cell number N4. Consequently, for cell D22 the formula will need to read:

+B22*100/N4

- Finally, use SUM to find the totals for this patient and print the details of the patient.

11.6 The Ice Cool Refrigerator Company

A group of partners are to set up a limited company for the purpose of manufacturing and selling refrigerators with start up Share Capital of £60,000 in the bank and an anticipated injection of further Share Capital from new shareholders once the business is under way.

The plans for the company are as follows:

- It will produce 120 gas fires a month but expects sales to start from 60 in July, increasing in steps of 20 each month until they reach 140 per month.

- The refrigerators will sell for £300 each but his customers' accounts will only be settled in the second month after the month of purchase.

- The overheads will be £5000 per month, paid one month in arrears.

- In September the business will pay £150,000 for equipment, machinery and computers needed to start up the business.

- In November, they expect to receive a further injection of Share Capital of £50,000.

- The unit production costs, which are not expected to rise in the period under review, will be as follows:

Materials	£90
Labour	£80
Variables	£40

- Materials will be bought as needed, with payment one month later. Labour will have to be paid for in the month of production as will variable costs. Interest charges on the previous month's overdraft will be debited at a rate of 1.5% per month.

In order to satisfy the bank manager that the request for additional funding of the business with an overdraft is reasonable, the business has been asked to draw up a cash flow forecast for the first six months of operations; that is from July until December.

- Use Lotus 123 to create the cash flow table that the bank manager will want to see before granting the overdraft facility asked for. The cash flow will also need to show the overdraft required.

- You should produce not only the print of the table as seen on the screen but also, in case the bank manager questions the derivation of the figures, a print showing the formulae used in it.

In October, the business finds that it is proceeding very much as had been planned and that advance orders suggest that sales are likely to be maintained at the December level during January and February, falling to 120 or 130 in March. This is extremely encouraging but leaves the business with the problem of how it is going to be able to satisfy the demand.

Production capacity of 120 gas fires a month has been sufficient to cope with the November/December demand but...

Overtime working, which will inevitably increase labour costs, seems to be called for and the business is to consider how this can be organised. The directors have already talked to staff and sufficient staff have said they would be willing to work overtime.

It is estimated that when production rises above 120 per month each refrigerator will add £40 to labour costs on each machine. Also, while the factory is working overtime, overheads will rise to £5,800 per month.

New machinery and maintenance costs of £12,000 will have to be paid for in April.

- Use Lotus 123 and with your existing model as a starting point, extend the analysis until June and investigate some of the possibilities. You may assume that only the labour cost and the added overheads will be affected by the overtime working and should remember that selling machines that have not been produced is not an acceptable means of improving cash flow.

- So that you have a record of the consequences of the alternative strategies you have investigated, you should print copies of the spreadsheets with sub-headings which indicate what strategy you were examining.

11.7 Hayley Computer Services

Hayley Computer Services Ltd is a small company offering computer consultancy and training to small businesses. The company has been trading for two years, the only staff being Mr James and his wife. Mr James is now worried that the £5,000 overdraft facility granted by his local bank manager will be insufficient to finance his company's modest expansion. To assist in his investigation of several possible plans, he has decided to set up a cash flow model covering the next 12 months.

Mrs James has made the following estimates for the year ending December 31, 1990;

- Fees received by the company in January 1990 will be £2,800 and these will rise steadily by 5% per month.

The company's expenses are expected to be:

- Rental of premises £400 in January – fixed for the year.

- General expenses of £500 in January, rising steadily by 3% a month.

- Fixed motor vehicle expenses of £100 per month.

- Wages and PAYE of £1,800 a month – fixed for 6 months but increased from July onwards by 25%.

In March Mr James intends changing his company car. He believes that he will be able to sell his present car for £5,600, and that the replacement will cost £7,900.

In September he expects to pay tax of £5,920 on the company's 1989 profits.

On January 1 1990 the company's bank account is expected to be £3,100 overdrawn.

You are required to:

1 Set up the model of the company's cash flow for the 12 months to December 31, 1990.

2 By modifying the basic model, ascertain the effect of each of the following proposals in turn on the company's overdraft position so that Mr James can decide which option is least likely to upset his bank manager.

a) A new issue of shares to Mr James' uncle giving a cash inflow of £4,200 in February 1990.

b) Taking out a loan of £4,000 in February to be repaid with £400 interest in December 1990.

c) Deferring the purchase of the new car for 12 months but facing extra running expenses of £40 a month after March 1990.

d) Paying £1,000 for advertising in January with an increase in sales of £200 a month (over and above the 5% growth) beginning in February and vacating his rented premises, working from home, from January 1990.

11.8 Employee sickness

This exercise requires you to perform the following tasks:

1 Load 123 into your computer and make sure you have a blank Sheet to work with.

2 Enter text on your spreadsheet to show a heading and a list of employee names as shown in screen dump 11.8.

```
A: A1: 'List of employees showing days lost for sickness                    READY

    A        A          B        C          D          E      F     G        H
1  List of employees showing days lost for sickness
2
3  Dates         From: 01-Jan-90      To:  01-Jan-91    No. of days   365
4
5  Employee Possible Sick days % lost
6
7   J Blue        205        10       4.88%
8   R Red         205         4       1.95%
9   T Gold        190         5       2.63%
10  K Pink        180         6       3.33%
11  F Green        80         0       0.00%
12  K Purple      190        25      13.16%
13  V Black       205         8       3.90%
14  G Orange      205        12       5.85%
15  A White       190         6       3.16%
16  H Brown       205         1       0.49%
17
18  Total working days               1855
19  Average days lost                3.94%
20  Standard deviation lost days     3.52%
21-Dec-90  10:35 PM
```

Screen Dump 11.8

3 Enter, for each employee, their number of days sickness and the number of possible days they could have.

4 Calculate the number of days between the two dates.

5 Use 123 facilities to calculate the percentage of days lost through sickness for each employee.

6 Calculate the total working days, an average percentage of days sickness and a standard deviation for sickness days.

Note: In order to tackle this you will need to know that Lotus 123 has a built in function for standard deviations:

@STD(List stating from .. to)

6 Get a printout of the table generated.

7 Alter some of the sick days figures and possible work days to make sure that the calculations work. Print out a second spreadsheet.

Such a spreadsheet might look like the one in screen dump 11.8.

11.9 Council house survey ──────────────

On examination of the sample spreadsheet in screen dump 11.9, it should be self evident about what is required from the survey.

```
A: A1: [W18] 'Use ot housing stock in the Borough of Watsit                    READY

     A           A        B     C     D     E     F     G     H        I
1    Use of housing stock in the Borough of Watsit
2    ─────────────────────────────────────────────────────────────────
3                       Number of occupants living in premises
4    ═════════════════════════════════════════════════════════════════
5                  CAT    1     2     3     4     5    6+     TOTALS
6    ─────────────────────────────────────────────────────────────────
7    1 bedroom flat   A    21    15     9     5     1     0        51
8    2 bedroom flat   B    19    13     9     5     3     1        50
9    3+ bedroom flat  C     5     5     8     7     1     1        27
10   1 bedroom house  D    79   187   154    90    41    10       561
11   2 bedroom house  E   111   199   211   123    39     9       692
12   3 bedroom house  F    32    76   110   110    60    12       400
13   4 bedroom house  G    10    11    17    15     9    10        72
14   5+ bedroom house H     1     2     3     2     2     2        12
15   ─────────────────────────────────────────────────────────────────
16           TOTALS      278   508   521   357   156    45      1865
17         PERCENTAGES    15%   27%   28%   19%    8%    2%      100%
18
19
20
22-Dec-90   09:37 AM
```

Screen Dump 11.9

The aim is to show the types of housing stock that exist within this fictitious council borough and the number of people living in the houses.

From the spreadsheet, you want to extract a number of bar charts (or pie charts) showing the distribution of the total housing among different types and how the number of occupants are distributed among each accommodation type. You will be able to produce a large number of charts with these figures.

Produce a number of charts displaying different aspects of data so that someone else can understand the data quickly and easily without having to read through the table.

When setting up a bar chart or pie chart, one of the problems you will face is trying to avoid a congested amount of information on the chart.

Such charts, therefore, should only be used when the number of categories are relatively small.

Note: To have more than one graph attached to a spreadsheet you will need to create different graph names. Also to print them, you will need to create graph files as well.

11.10 Price lists for a transport company _____

Examine screen dump 11.10 showing the transport company's price list before starting this exercise.

```
A: A1:                                                              READY

    A       A        B           C       D       E       F       G
                            PRICE LIST FOR VEHICLE TRANSPORT FOR
 1                              HITEC TRANSPORT CO. LTD.
 2
 3
 4                              Motor   Car     Van     Lorry
 5                              Cycle
 6   Cost in pence per mile (p)  21.50   27.00   36.50   51.00
 7  ---------------------------------------------------------------
 8   COUNTY   TOWN        MILES   Motor   Car     Van     Lorry
 9                                Cycle
10
11   Cornwall Penzance    292.00   62.78   78.84  106.58  148.92
12   Cornwall Falmouth    282.00   60.63   76.14  102.93  143.82
13   Cornwall Truro       271.00   58.27   73.17   98.92  138.21
14   Devon    Exeter      172.00   36.98   46.44   62.78   87.72
15   Devon    Plymouth    216.00   46.44   58.32   78.84  110.16
16   Devon    Torbay      198.00   42.57   53.46   72.27  100.98
17   Somerset Taunton     167.00   35.91   45.09   60.96   85.17
18   Somerset Yeovil      128.00   27.52   34.56   46.72   65.28
19   Avon     Weston-S-Mare 143.00  30.75   38.61   52.20   72.93
20   Avon     Bristol     120.00   25.80   32.40   43.80   61.20
22-Dec-90  09:48 AM
```

Screen Dump 11.10

From observation you will see that there is a heading for county and a town within that county. The mileage indicates the number of miles from the town to London.

The costs indicate the cost per mile for running each vehicle type (in pence). For each town, therefore, the cost of running a vehicle from London to the stated town is calculated. The use of such a spreadsheet allows a new price list to be easily and quickly constructed each time the prices per mile change.

1 Construct such a list for England, Wales, Scotland or any other country by having every county (province or state) represented by between TWO and FOUR of the principle towns or cities. You will need a map of the country with mileage from a given focal point (London in this example) to the town or city.

For each country, produce two lists with the following costs:

	first list	second list
Motor Cycle	18p	21p
Car	32p	34p
Van	36p	33p
Truck	57p	55p

2 If you are a Release 3 user, then copy the entire spreadsheet on to another sheet and rearrange the list on one of the sheets showing list in county alphabetical order. For Release 2 users, rearrange the existing list in county alphabetical order.

3 Repeat task 2 with list in town alphabetical order. Release 3 users will need to create a third sheet.

4 Again, repeating task 3, produce a list in distance order (furthest distance first). Alter the mileage costs for this example.

Note: The total costs for each vehicle should be in currency format.

If a county does not have four major towns, place as many in the list as you can.

The whole width of the spreadsheet should be visible on the screen. You will need to use sensible abbreviations where required.

11.11 Football League tables _____

This spreadsheet is designed to show a Football League championship table, or any other equivalent application, in such a way that ensures the club with the highest number of points appears at the top of the table.

Part of the table takes the form of the one shown in screen dump 11.11.

```
A: A1: [W12]                                                          READY

   A    A          B      C      D      E      F      G      H      I
1                        LEAGUE CHAMPIONSHIP TABLE
2
3               Played   Won    Lost   Drawn  Goals  Goals  Goal   Points
4                                             for    Against Diff
5    Arsenal        19    13     1      5      29     8      21     44
6    Totenham       19    11     1      7      30     9      21     40
7    Liverpool      19    11     1      7      25     5      20     40
8    Leeds          19     9     2      8      18     8      10     35
9    Chelsea        19     9     3      7      18     13      5     34
10   Man City       19     8     4      7      16     15      1     31
11   Man Utd        19     8     5      6      16     16      0     30
12   Coventry       19     6     5      8      11     18     -7     26
13   Everton        19     8    10      1      16     21     -5     25
14   Sheff. Utd     19     6     7      6      12     20     -8     24
15   Wimbledon      19     5     8      6      10     22    -12     21
16   Luton          19     4     7      8       8     22    -14     20
17   Crystal Pal.   19     4     7      8       8     22    -14     20
18   Southampton    19     3     6     10       6     22    -16     19
19   Notts For      19     1    11      7       2     29    -27     10
20   Wimbledon      19     1    13      5       5     31    -26      8
22-Dec-90   12:28 PM
```

Screen Dump 11.11

Note:

the points system is   Win = 3 points
                       Draw = 1 point

Played = Won + Lost + Drawn

Goal Diff = (goals for) - (goals against)

If two clubs have the same number of points, then the greater goal difference determines the higher club.

1   Produce a spreadsheet for this table

2   At the foot of the table show the following:

    1   Number of clubs

    2   Highest number of wins

    3   Highest number of defeats

    4   Average number of goals for

    5   Average number of goals against

    6   The league leader

All the figures at the foot of the table should be calculated by the spreadsheet program and not entered by you.

11.12 World weather chart

This spreadsheet sets out a world weather chart to show the temperature in different locations throughout the world as shown in screen dump 11.12.

```
A: A11:                                                    READY

     A      A       B     C      D          E        F      G        H          I
  1
  2
  3                            WORLD WEATHER
  4             ------------------------------------------------------
  5
  6             C     F                          C      F
  7    Aberdeen  19    66          Leeds        18     64
  8    Algiers   24    75          Lisbon       22     72
  9    Bristol   17    63          London       17     63
 10    Cardiff   17    63          Manchester   18     64
 11
 12
 13
 14
 15
 16
 17
 18
 19
 20
 22-Dec-90  12:34 PM
```

Screen Dump 11.12

NB C = Centigrade   :   F = Fahrenheit

1 Design a spreadsheet to display this information. Include your own data taken from newspapers or invented. The temperature in Fahrenheit can be found from the temperature in Centigrade as:

Fahrenheit = (Centigrade * 1.8) + 32

2 At the foot of the table, show:

The average temperatures
The number of locations
The name of the hottest place
The name of the coldest place

All these figures should be calculated and not added by you.

11.13 Car burglar alarm explosion _____

This spreadsheet requires you to set out the components of a car
burglar alarm that is to be produced by a small engineering company.
The final product will be in 'black box form' ready to install into a
car. The objective of this exercise is to calculate, at component level,
the cost of materials and production of the alarm in order to derive a
profitable selling price.

```
A: A19:                                                      READY

    A              B            C       D        E        F
1  CAR BURGLAR ALARM EXPLOSION RECORD
2  ------------------------------------------------------------
3                               No.     Suppl.   Unit
4                               Req     Code     Price
    A              B            C       D        E        F
5  Resistors
6  R1.2          2k2            2       M2K2     0.04
7  R3            10k            1       M10K     0.04
8  R4            75R (0.5W)     1       S75R     0.04
9
10 Capacitors
11 C1            1000uf         1       FB82D    0.18
12 C2            2200uf         1       FB90X    0.53
13 C3            470uf          1       FB72P    0.16
14
15 Semi-Conductors
16 TR1.2         BC161          1       QL49D    0.24
17 TR3           BC108          1       QL32K    0.19
18 D1            IN4001         1       QL73Q    0.56
19
22-Dec-90   03:43 PM                                      CAPS
```

Screen Dump 11.13a

From the list, shown in screen dumps 13.13a and 13b, you should be
able to enter the number of alarm systems you wish to make and the
spreadsheet will then produce a 'shopping list' giving a list of
components needed and their costs along with a total cost. It is
suggested, therefore, that your spreadsheet has the following sections:

- A component breakdown, per alarm, as shown above

- A column to hold costs of multiple components; for example, $10 \times$
0.4w metal film 2K2

- An entry for the desired number of 'final product' car alarm(s)

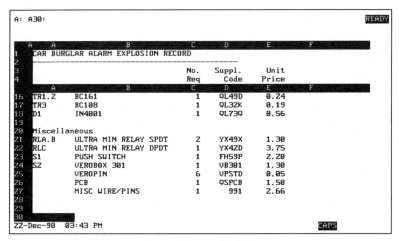

A: A30:						READY

Screen Dump 11.13b

- A list of total components needed, with unit costs, in alphabetical order

Try taking advantage of macros in order to sort the list by cost as well in as component order. Also, use a macro to simplify the printing of each section.

You will find the use of a horizontal useful because the spreadsheet has more rows of infomation than can be seen on the screen at any one time.

12 A REFERENCE GUIDE

12.1 Aims of this chapter _____

This chapter should be used as a reference guide in that it lists all the commands available in Lotus 123 with a sentence explaining their function. The tree diagram of the menu structure of Lotus will help you find your way around the package.

Quite often you will find that things go wrong, especially in the earlier stages. In most cases what appears alarming is relatively simple to put right. The concluding section of this chapter assists you in detecting errors and faults and offers some suggestion as to how they can be put right.

12.2 Menu structure _____

For the menu diagrams an asterisk (*) has been placed next to an option to indicate that the option is not available to Lotus Release 2 users.

The main menu in table 12.1 shows there are 10 command sub-menus.

Table 12.1

1 Worksheet _____
General purpose: To perform general changes on the way the spreadsheet is presented. This section of the commands is extensive and has the sections as shown in table 12.2.

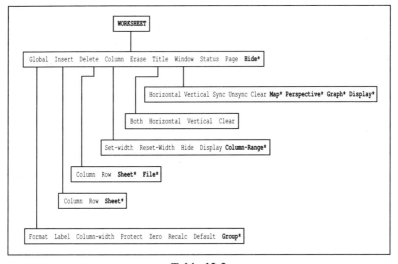

Table 12.2

There are ten commands in this menu:

(a) Global performs changes throughout the whole spreadsheet

(b) Insert inserts a blank row, column or another spreadsheet

(c) Delete deletes a row, column, sheet or file

(d) Column allows the widening or narrowing of columns. Also used to hide columns from visible display

(e) Erase erases the whole spreadsheet

(f) Title holds the top row and left column so that they remain visible wherever you are in the spreadsheet

(g) Window partitions the screen so that you see different sections of you spreadsheets

(h) Status displays technical information about your spreadsheet

(i) Page creates page breaks in sheets for printing purposes

(j) Hide hides complete spreadsheets

Of the Worksheet, Global options there are eight further options:

(a) Format sets all spreadsheet cells to a given format

(b) Label sets text left, right or centred in cell

(c) Column-width sets default column width; it is 9 on start

(d) Protect stops writing to cells

(e) Zero a blank cell shows when the value in a cell is zero

(f) Recalc sets automatic recalculation on all spreadsheets

(g) Default changes everything back to 123 defaults

(h) Group makes all spreadsheets obey the same format

2 Range

General purpose: To perform a change on a range of cells in the spreadsheet. Table 12.3 shows how the commands are structured.

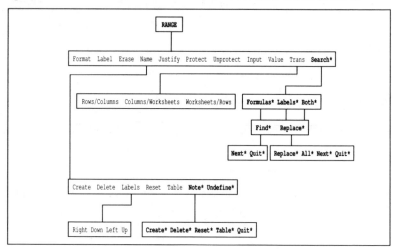

Table 12.3

Format, Label, Erase, Protect and Unprotect are exactly the same as for Worksheet Global except that they work on a range of cells rather than on a whole spreadsheet (or group of spreadsheets if set).

3 Copy

General purpose: To copy a range of cells from one part of a spreadsheet to another part.

4 Move

General purpose: To move a range of cells from one part of a spreadsheet to another part.

5 File

General purpose: To manipulate files stored on disk.

For most purposes, you will only use Save and Retrieve. A knowledge of your computer's operating system and the way in which is configured will you get the most out of this. Table 12.4 shows how it is structured.

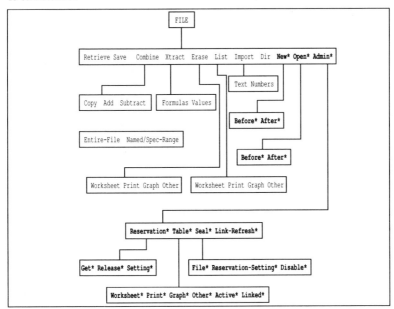

Table 12.4

6 Print

General purpose: To manipulate your printer for printed output.

One of the main differences between Release 2 and 3 printing is the fact that Release 3 can print a graph without leaving the spreadsheet and calling on another program and the fact that Release 3 can print a spreadsheet sideways on paper (landscape) rather then simply top down (portrait).

A knowledge of your printer type will help you get the most out of this. Table 12.5 shows how it is structured.

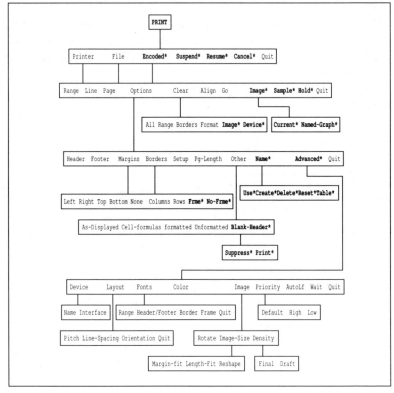

Table 12.5

The use of encoded allows you to store the settings so that you do not have to keep changing all your printer settings, such as margins and page lengths, every time you load Lotus into your computer. Printing can always be suspended while you change paper in your printer and resumed later. Also, you can cancel the printing at any time.

Sending printed output to a file allows you to process the file later with another software package.

Many of the advanced features will require some numbers to be entered. Not all printers are capable of all options. You will need to experiment with this in order to get an idea of what your printer can do.

7 Graph

General purpose: To produce, display and save a graph of your spreadsheet information.

The extent to which you can show graphs on screens is dependent largely on the type of screen you have. This will have been set up when the package was installed. Also, what can be printed is dependent upon the type of printer you have.

Table 12.6 overleaf shows the structure of the graphing commands.

8 Data

General purpose: To manipulate data stored in database tables. Table 12.7 outlines the command structure.

The Data commands are grouped into nine categories:

(a) Fill enters a sequence of values into range. Typically, it allows you to number your records

(b) Table creates a table that shows how results of formulae change when you change the numbers used in the formulae

(c) Sort sorts a range of data into a specified order

(d) Query locates and allows editing of specified records

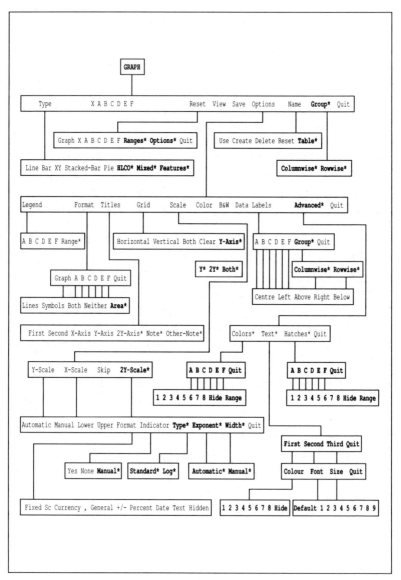

Table 12.6

(e) Distribution sets up a frequency distribution of the values in a range that fall within specified number intervals

(f) Matrix inverts or multiplies matrices made up of rows and columns of numbers

(g) Regression performs regression analysis by comparing the relationship between sets of numbers

(h) Parse separates and converts a single column of labels into several columns of data

(i) External links Lotus 123 to an external table

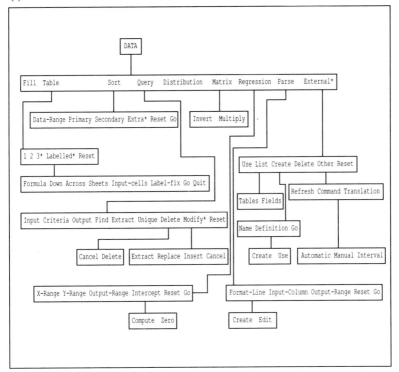

Table 12.7

9 System

General purpose: To get into the operating system to use DOS commands. When you are in the system you can return from where you left off by entering EXIT.

10 Quit

General purpose: To leave the spreadsheet program. You will be warned as a way of reminding that anything not saved will be lost.

12.3 Fault finding and error messages

One of the first ways of detecting an error is when the mode indicator at the top right of the screen states 'ERROR'. When this happens, press the F1 key (the HELP function) to reveal the nature of the error. Some of the most common errors that are shown are:

Printer errors

This normally occurs because the printer is not ready. Check out the following:

● Has it been switched on?

● Is it connected to the computer?

● Has the printer run out of paper?

Remember, if the correct printer has not been installed, then printing is unlikely to be successful. If you change your printer, then run the Install program and select the options that allow you to change the device types.

Disk errors

Typical ones are:

● A disk is not in the drive from which you are attempting to read. You are trying to access the wrong disk directory.

● You are using the wrong file name.

● The file or disk is corrupt. There is often little you can do when this type of problems occurs.

- There is insufficient room on a disk to store the file you want to save. In this instance, simply use another disk.

- The file you are trying to read or combine with is not compatible with your version of Lotus 123.

Memory errors

These errors occur if your computer has insufficient memory to cope with the size of spreadsheet you want to handle. In your early stages of spreadsheet handling, this is unlikely to occur. As a matter of policy, it is always better to set a few smaller spreadsheets rather than very large ones; smaller problems are easier to handle!

'ERR' appearing in a cell

This indicates that Lotus cannot derive the value in that cell. This normally happens because a formula or function is trying to calculate a figure with a non-numeric cell value or range. Alternatively, you could be trying to divide a number by zero.

It can also occur if, after setting up a formula, you then move some of the data that is needed by the formula. As a result of doing this, ERR cells appear often in unexpected places. In this case check the formulae.

Upper and lower case

In some cases, the functions or commands can be case sensitive. In other words, the word 'Monday' is quite different to the word 'MONDAY' because of the difference in case. This can cause a problem when setting up conditions in the database facilities or when using conditional IF statements.

12.4 The function keys

Lotus makes extensive use of the function keys on your keyboard which can act as useful ways of saving time and making matters easier. The basic ones are:

F1   Help screen.

F2   Edit a cell.

F3   Lists the Named ranges created in your spreadsheet. This is used when working with menus.

F4   Adjusts a cell or range of cell formulae between Absolute, relative and mixed references.

F5   Goto. Allows you to jump straight to a specified cell.

F6   Allows you to jump between windows that have been set up.

F7   This repeats the most recent QUERY command that was used in the Database features of Lotus.

F8   Repeats the last Data Table command selected.

F9   Recalculates formulae in all active cells.

F10   Displays your graph.

Lotus also has further use of function keys where you have to press the 'Alt' key on your keyboard and the respective Function key simultaneously.

ALT-F1   Allows the creation of characters in cells that cannot be created by simply typing them in.

ALT-F2   Allows you to use the contents of a record buffer.

ALT-F3   Allows you to select a macro to run.

ALT-F4   Allows you to UNDO anything since the READY mode indicator was last on. When Lotus is first set up the UNDO feature is off and you are unable to use this. Using ALT-F4 before you use a command will switch it on.

ALT-F5   Not used.

ALT-F6   Enlarges a current Sheet when working with multiple sheets in the PERSPECTIVE mode.

ALT-F7, ALT-F8 and ALT-F9 are used with Lotus Release 3 Add-In special extension features.

12.5 The label prefixes

These are used to indicate that the entry into a cell is a label. The ones available are:

'   Left justified in cell

"   Right justified in cell

^   Centred in cell

\   Repeated in cell

12.6 The logical operators

These are used in formulae to help decision making with the @IF function. The ones available are:

=	equal to
<	less than
>	greater than
>=	less than or equal to
>=	greater than or equal to
<>	not equal to
#AND#	Logical AND. For example if a cell has the function:

@IF(C1 "SMITH" #AND# C2 >= 18,"yes,'no)

then it reads 'if the contents of cell C1 is not SMITH and cell C2 is greater than or equal to 18 then place 'yes' into cell right justified or else place 'no' into the cell left justified.

#NOT#	Logical NOT and works in the same manner as #AND#.
#OR#	Logical OR and works in the same manner as #AND#.

12.7 Date and time formats _____

Lotus dates and times can be formatted in a number of ways

	Format	Example
Dates	DD-MMM-YY	25-Dec-91
	DD-MMM	25-Dec
	MMM-YY	Dec-91
	Long Intn'l	12/25/91
	Short Intn'l	12/25

Both Long Intn'l and Short Intn'l (MM/DD/YY and MM/DD) use American date expressions rather than European date formats (DD/MM/YY).

Lotus times can be expressed in one of four ways:

	Format	Example
Times	HH:MM:SS AM/PM	4:45:51 PM
	HH:MM AM/PM	4:45 PM
	Long Intn'l	16:45:51
	Short Intn'l	16:45

Basically you have the choice of a 12 or 24 hour clock with or without seconds.

GLOSSARY

Abort Stopping a program or operation while it is still running.

Absolute cell address When setting up a formula in a cell, the use of the dollar ($) sign allows copying of formula without such a cell reference being altered. For example, if a formula had an absolute cell reference of $B$12, the cell reference of B12 will remain the same when copied to other cells.

Access The activity of referring to data stored in a file. For example, when working in a Lotus 123 spreadsheet, you may need to access a file for combining data or simply to work with a saved spreadsheet.

Access menu The Lotus 123 start up menu.

Amend The activity of changing a file. For example, altering an existing spreadsheet.

Anchoring A process of moving the cursor to a cell to start highlighting a range of cells.

Applications package A specific use to which a computer is put. Lotus 123 is an example of such an applications package.

ASCII An anacronym for American Standard Code for Information Interchange. It is a form of TEXT data that can be stored on disk that most applications can read.

Background printing A process where the computer prints a document and still allows you to use the computer for something else. This facility is not available in Lotus 123 when used with MSDOS.

Backing storage The principle of storing data such as disks for long term storage purposes. Lotus 123 software comes on such backing storage media.

Backup A process of copying all data from one source to another for safe keeping. Backup files are often denoted by the file extension '.BAK'.

Bar chart or graph A Lotus graph using vertical bars spaced along the X-Axis to depict data.

Batch processing The activity of grouping transactions together and then processing them all in one go. For example, a spreadsheet may have been set up which requires large data input of, say, sales details. Rather than entering place details on as they are received, you may decide to enter all details at pre-defined times in the week.

Blank cell A cell with no data in it.

Bootstrap A small program built into the computer that instructs the system about how to set itself up when switched on. Part of the bootstrap is often held on the hard disk which is needed when your machine is switched on.

Buffer A part of memory used as a temporary store to hold data from an input device. For example, most printers have a buffer memory for storing data prior to printing it. It means your printer will go on printing a spreadsheet after Lotus has sent the details to your printer. Also keyboards often hold at least one line of data before it is sent to the computer's processor. Data from a keyboard will be sent to the computer after the Return or Enter key has been pressed.

Bug An error in a program, macro or spreadsheet.

Byte A measure of computer memory containing 8 single bits. Each byte often represents a single character. 1024 of these bytes is a kilobyte.

Carriage return A single character sent to the computer by pressing the RETURN key on the keyboard. In Lotus carriage returns are used to release data from the keyboard to the spreadsheet via the computer's processor.

Cell An element of the worksheet where data is entered. Such cells are addressed by a reference and are organised in a grid pattern of rows and columns. Cell can be formatted for various displays and with differing widths.

Central processing unit Usually referred to as simply the processor or microprocessor, it is the main unit of any computer system. The processor accepts its data from input devices, processes such data and sends it to output devices such as screens and printers, or sends it to backing store for saving. Lotus interacts with it all the time it is operative.

Character A single element in coded form for the processor, such as a letter or a single number digit. Such characters are normally 8 bits or one byte long.

Clock A processor contains an electronic pulse generator that is used to transmit such synchronised pulses to different parts of the computer for the interpretation and execution of instructions. Such synchronisation will be set at a speed that determines the computer's CLOCK SPEED. Such clock speeds are measured in Megahertz (MHz). The faster the clock speed, the faster the internal processing speed of the computer. This becomes apparent when working with large spreadsheets or multiple spreadsheets in Lotus.

Column A vertical block of cells in the spreadsheet of 8192 cells. Columns are referred to by letters of the alphabetic from A to Z and then AA..AZ, BA..BZ and so on. Lotus allows the use of 256 such columns.

Command An instruction to the computer to perform a given task. A Lotus command is activated through its menu structure or with a function key.

Control panel The top three lines of the Lotus screen contain the control panel. It is needed to see what is happening in the spreadsheet and guide you through the commands.

Corruption A term used to refer to the loss or corruption of data. If it occurs on a disk it usually renders such data as useless. If this happens, then it might require you to install Lotus again or restore a backup of files.

Criteria Used in the Lotus database routines to set up rules or matchings under which records are located, copied or deleted.

Cursor   A small image in the form of a block or dash on the screen to indicate which cell data will be entered from the keyboard or what command is being used.

Daisy wheel printer   A printer that prints characters by striking the character images on carbonated ribbon. The characters appear on the end of spokes on a small wheel. Such printers are unable to print Lotus graphs and some of the Lotus special fonts.

Data   An element of information that will need processing to form the basis of information. When working with Lotus, you will place such data into cells leaving Lotus to process the data further in accordance with a set of commands.

Database   The collection, in a structured form, of records. Lotus represents a database in a table of records where each row in the database table becomes a record.

Date format   The way in which Lotus displays a date in a cell.

Default   When offering a choice to users through Lotus, a default value is assumed if no choice is made. For example, Lotus sets cell widths at a default of 9 characters which remain unless changed by you.

Directory   A part of the disk where files can be stored. A disk will have many such directories which are used for storing different kinds of files. Organising files into directories is an important part of data management and works rather like organising files in a filing cabinet.

Disk   Magnetic storage medium used to store data. Such data will be organised into files and given file names for easy identification.

Disk Drive   A device for storing data generated by the Lotus and for retrieving data by Lotus. Disk drives can contain either floppy disks or hard disks.

DOS (Disk Operating System)   Part of the software that is contained on disk, loaded into computer memory and used to operate the computer system.

Download The process of loading Lotus into computer memory or loading a Lotus file into a spreadsheet.

Driver A part of the Operating System software that is used to control certain devices such as a printer.

Encoded file A Lotus file used to store special characteristics about your printer. It is created using the command sequence /Print, Encoded.

Error message A signal telling you that Lotus has either detected an error with equipment or cannot perform a certain task.

Field An element of a record that is a collection of characters stored in a single cell such as that which makes up a customer name or stock number.

File A collection of data stored on the disk, such as all the data making up a spreadsheet. Such files will have unique names within directories.

File protection A method of protecting files from corruption or accidental erasure. A common way of protecting a file is to write protect it, which means files can be read but not written to.

Floppy disk A backing store medium used to store data. Such disks require a disk drive in order for the computer to read from them and write to them. Lotus is dispatched on such floppy disks and has to be installed on to a hard disk.

Font A style of print that appears on your printer or screen.

Form feed A process where a printer feeds a sheet of paper through the printer. This is often used to align continuous paper on a printer to the top of the next sheet.

Format The way data is structured on disk paper or screens. It is a very general term that Lotus uses to describe the way information is presented to you on screen or paper.

Function A built-in Lotus formula that performs a specific task.

Function key A set of keys on your keyboard used to perform certain tasks. A list of the function keys appears in chapter 12.

Graph files These are files of stored graphs. In Release 2 they are needed for printing and have a '.PIC' extension to them. Release 3 files have a '.CGM' extension as default and are normally needed when used with other programs.

Handshaking A process where both computer and a device, such as your printer tell each other that data is ready to be sent. A printer requires this because it is normally unable to print data as fast as it can receive it, so the principle of handshaking ensures data are sent down as and when the printer is ready, thereby preventing loss of data.

Hard copy Printed output from your computer.

Hardware The physical attributes of your computer system.

Housekeeping A term to describe the practice of keeping unwanted information on disks. Good housekeeping will prevent disks and directories from becoming cluttered. It will help you save time in the long run.

Icon A pictorial representation of programs, document files and options available for executing or processing. Icons are often used as an alternative to text menus and directories. Lotus does not use such icons, but many operating systems do.

If statement A conditional statement used in a Lotus function, @IF. It allows Lotus to make some decisions on various outcomes.

Impact printers A category of printer that creates images on paper by physically hitting the paper such as matrix.

Input-Range The range specified when performing a Data Query on a Data Table.

Install program A Lotus program that installs your Lotus software onto disk.

Interface A general term used to describe the processing of data between two systems or sub-systems. For example, a disk interface refers to the process of transferring data from processor to disk and back. Such interfaces are collections of both hardware and software.

Job In a computing context, this refers to either routines or applications being run on a computer system at any one point in time. Running the Lotus package is an example of a Job while printing its spreadsheet is another.

Keyboard One of the most used forms of input devices.

Kilobyte (K) Used to measure data quantity and represents 1024 bytes of data.

Label Any cell entry the begins with a letter or is prefixed with one of the label prefixes. Chapter 12 has a list of them.

Laser printer A non-impact printer giving high quality printed output. Its technology is based on similar techniques that of photocopiers.

Legend Explanation of the variables used in graphs. Such legends are needed if other people are to be able to interpret the meaning of your graphs.

Line graph A Lotus graph showing variables represented as lines.

Line printer Low quality, very high speed printers that print complete lines at a time.

Local Area Network (LAN) A system that connects a number of microcomputers so that they can share common resources such as a printer. While resources can be shared, each computer on a network is still able to act independently of each other. Lotus will work on a network, but you will need to be careful when using spreadsheets that others are using at the same time.

Logical operator Used in formulae to help decision making with the @IF function. Chapter 12 has a list of them.

Logging in A method of getting access to a computers information. Designed for security, the process of logging would require you to enter identification and an associated password. This process is most likely when you use a network or multi-user system.

Macro A set of Lotus instructions stored and capable of being called up by depressing the ALT key with a single letter simultaneously.

Magnetic disks A storage medium for data which fits into a disk drive.

Main menu The first menu that appears in the Lotus control panel when you depress the '/' key.

Matrix printer An impact printer that creates an image on paper through a dot pattern on a matrix. Such matrix printers are effective for printing graphics as well as near letter quality text. Such printers are often quite adequate for most uses and Lotus is capable of making full use of nearly all matrix printers on the market.

Menu A set of commands that appears in the control panel.

Microprocessor The common name given to the processing unit of a microcomputer.

Mixed cell address A formula contained in a cell where part of the formula uses an absolute cell address while other parts are relative. The dollar ($) sign is used to determine whether a cell formula or function has an absolute address. For example the cell contents

'+($C12-D12)/$F$12'

show C is absolute in C12 and when copied will remain as C while the 12 could change. F12 will remain as F12 while copying. Cell D12 will change when the formula is copied.

Mode indicator This is situated in the top right-hand corner of the screen and is used to inform what mode Lotus is in. For example, if it states READY it is waiting for input while if it states MENU it waiting for a menu command.

Modulator/Demodulator (MODEM) A device for both sending and receiving data between computers down a telephone line. This would allow you to transmit spreadsheets between computers in a very short time. A modem will be needed at both ends of a line to allow data communication to work.

MSDOS A trade name for Microsoft Disk Operating System.

Named graph A graph saved within a Lotus spreadsheet. The purpose of naming graphs is to allow you to have a large number of them for one spreadsheet.

Numeric value A number stored in cell or the result of a formula.

Off-Line A general term referring to data or part of computer system being inaccessible. In other words, data on a disk which is not in the computer disk drive is said to be off-line. Storing spreadsheets on floppy disk and removing the disk from the drive will render your data off-line.

Operating system Software that is used to operate the computer and its devices.

Orientation A process of turning a graph or printed output around 90% so that it better display the information for a particular application.

OS/2 Operating System/2 is an operating system for which Lotus release 3 and release 3.1 will work on. The operating system allows multi-tasking; doing more than one operation at a time.

Output-Range A range where Lotus can place records after a Data Query operation has been made.

Path This refers to the directory route to which files are set. If a file is stored as C:\123\motors.wk3, then its path is \123 on C drive.

Peripheral device Input, Output and Storage devices of a computer that form part of your system hardware.

Perspective view A view of three sheets of spreadsheet on the screen at the same time. It is presented in a layered effect of one sheet appearing on top of the other.

Pie chart A circular chart showing how a variable is broken up proportionately.

Pointer The process of highlighting a cell or a menu command. The arrow keys are used to move the pointer.

Print file A file where printer output is stored. These files have the extension '.PRN' at the end of them and can be used by other programs, in particular a word processor.

Prompt A message to you on the screen indicating that input is wanted.

RAM–Random Access Memory This is a part of the computer's memory that is needed to store both Lotus and the spreadsheets you use and prepare.

Range A rectangular block of cells either highlighted or named.

Read/Write heads A device contained within a disk drive or tape drive that either reads data into the computer or writes data on to a storage medium from the computer. These heads are normally well protected, but can be damaged if sufficient care of your computer is not taken.

Record A collection of cells in a row of a database table.

Relative cell address See mixed cell addressing.

Reset To clear a setting or restore to the Lotus default setting.

Retrieve The process of loading a stored spreadsheet into Lotus.

ROM (Read Only Memory) A part of the memory in a computer used to store programs in a permanent way. This ROM is needed to store part of the computer's operating system.

Root directory The main directory of a disk. When Lotus is installed, you will normally store all the files generated in sub-directory.

Row Horizontal row of cells. Each row has 256 cells and is numbered. Lotus allows the use of up to 8192 rows.

Run The actual execution of a program.

Save The process of storing your spreadsheet into a file on disk.

Scrolling A process of text running up and down the screen when you want to view data past the bottom of the screen or across the screen when data is past the right of left of the screen. The arrow keys allow this scrolling.

Setup string a collection of characters preceded with the \ symbol stored to control the printer. The string is set up by the command sequence /Print, Printer, Options, Other, Setup.

Soft copy A term used for screen output.

Software All computer programs from operating system to applications software.

Sort A term used when rearranging records in a data table into a different order.

Stacked-bar chart Each bar of a bar graph is split up into sections showing how a variable is broken up in proportions.

Stand-alone system A computer that is capable of working in isolation from any other system. Most microcomputers are stand-alone systems.

Storage capacity A way of measuring the amount of data that can be stored. Storage capacity is normally measured in Kilobytes (K).

String A collection of characters stored as a label.

Sub-directory A directory leading off another directory. If your files are stored in the directory C:\123R3\DATA*.WK3, then 123R3 is a sub-directory to the root directory and DATA is a sub-directory to the 123R3 directory.

Tilde (~) A character on the keyboard which is used in a macro to indicate Enter or Return.

Translate utility A program that comes with the Lotus package that can be used to translate spreadsheet files of one program or version of Lotus to another. The Translate program can be used from the Lotus Access screen.

Unix An operating system associated with minicomputers or large multi-user microcomputers. The operating system is a standard that is used on many different models of machines and is not associated with one particular manufacturer.

User friendly A term often associated with the way software guides a user through processes when using a computer applications package. Because Lotus is not used for a specific purpose such as accounts, many people regard it as not very user friendly. However, you will have made your own mind up about whether you think Lotus is user friendly.

Utility program   A program that can be used to manage files or perform activities outside the normal scope of running a program such as backing up files, retrieving lost files and creating directories.

Value   A number or the outcome of a formula.

Variable   A part of a formula for which other values will substitute. Such variables will change when other numbers change.

Visual Display Unit (VDU)   The screen that displays text and graphic output as soft copy.

Winchester Drive   A storage device that holds a hard disk. The hard disk is non-removable but offers high storage density and capacity and is generally very reliable.

Wildcard character or symbol   A character used to represent any single character or set of character. Lotus uses the asterisk (*) for a number of characters and the question mark (?) for a single character. When you see the file *.WK? listed it means all files with the extension .WK followed by any single character.

Window   A method of sectioning the VDU in such a way that an operator can see different parts of a document or run and see different applications at the same time.

Word processing   An application that involves processing words and spending time perfecting format, spelling and so on before producing hard copy. Lotus spreadsheets can be output in a way that word processors can incorporate them into other documents.

Worksheet A   Lotus word for spreadsheet.

Xenix   An operating associated with large multi-user microcomputers. The operating system is a standard that is used on many different models of machines and is not associated with one particular manufacturer.

XY graphs   These are scatter graphs that show the relationship between two variables. Each point appears on the graph as a dot to establish any correlation.